THE REALLY, REALLY

REALLY EASY
STEP-BY-STEP
COMPUTER
BOOK 2 (XP)

for novice to intermediate users of all ages

This edition published in 2007 by New Holland Publishers (UK) Ltd
London · Cape Town · Sydney · Auckland
Garfield House, 86-88 Edgware Road, London W2 2EA, United Kingdom
80 McKenzie Street, Cape Town 8001, South Africa
Unit 1, 66 Gibbes Street, Chatswood, NSW 2067, Australia
218 Lake Road, Northcote, Auckland, New Zealand

First published in 2007 by
Struik Publishers
(a division of New Holland Publishing (South Africa) (Pty) Ltd)

www.newhollandpublishers.com

2 4 6 8 10 9 7 5 3 1

Publishing Manager: Linda de Villiers
Managing Editor: Cecilia Barfield
Editor and Indexer: Irma van Wyk
Designer: Janine Damon
Illustrator: Cheryl Smith
Proofreader: Joy Clack
Series concept: Gavin Hoole

Reproduction by Hirt & Carter Cape (Pty) Ltd
Printed and bound by Kyodo Printing Co (Singapore) Pte Ltd

ISBN 978 1 84537 792 2

Over 40 000 unique African images available to purchase
from our image bank at www.imagesofafrica.co.za

Contents

Read this before you start

THIS BOOK IS A SEQUEL TO COMPUTER BOOK 1 (XP)

Computer Book 2 (XP), as its title suggests, follows on from Computer Book 1 (XP).
It assumes you already know some basic procedures, such as:

- switching the computer on and turning it off in the correct manner;
- opening, minimizing, maximizing and closing programs and windows;
- creating, saving and printing documents using Microsoft Office Word, and using some of the basic text formatting tools in Word;
- copying, cutting and pasting items;
- connecting to the Internet and exploring Web sites;
- sending and receiving e-mail, including attachments; and
- using some popular keyboard and Toolbar shortcuts.

If you're not yet familiar with these procedures then we recommend that you work your way through Computer Book 1 (XP) before continuing with Book 2 (XP).

Book 2 (XP) takes the absolute beginner to the next level: novice and intermediate. The detailed step-by-step approach used in Book 1 (XP) has therefore been streamlined slightly here and there in order to reflect the user's progress from knowing absolutely nothing to being somewhat conversant with and competent in the basics.

Lastly, this is a book that helps a user achieve things with a computer; it is not intended to be an in-depth educational treatise on computers. It's for the majority of users who don't want a lot of waffle but simply want to know how they can do the things that are considered to be the most important or most popular needs of the typical computer user. Specialized programs such as accounting, graphic design, games and so on are not what this book is about.

THE USER-FRIENDLY VISUAL SYSTEM

We've used the same user-friendly visual system as we did in Book 1 (XP), which makes it really, really, really easy for anyone to enjoy learning how to do things on a personal computer.

Colour-coded windows are used throughout the book so that you can see at a glance the *type* of information you're looking at:

- introductions and explanations in normal black text on a white background;

- step-by-step procedures in yellow boxes;

- hints and tips in blue boxes;

- **very important notes and warnings in boxes with red borders.**

The detailed procedures are supported where necessary by pictures (screenshots) of the computer screen or the program window to clarify what you'll see on your screen.

WHICH VERSION OF WINDOWS ARE YOU USING?
This book is based on the Windows XP operating system. If you're using a different version of Windows or of any of the various Microsoft programs used in this book – or perhaps other brands of programs – then you'll need to adapt as appropriate.

DIALOG BOXES

When working in programs and selecting actions, Windows will often open a *dialog box* offering you various options.

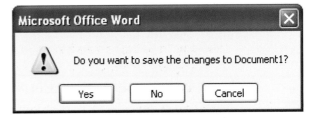

A simple dialog box

ALWAYS READ THE DIALOG BOX INFO
Always read the info in a dialog box before clicking on anything or pressing Enter .
This will help you avoid selecting a wrong action and having to fix it afterwards.

GETTING OUT OF TROUBLE

Don't be afraid to experiment. If the wrong window pops up on your screen you can usually get back to where you were by pressing the Esc key on your keyboard, or by using the mouse to click on the **Cancel** button in the unwanted open dialog box.

CREATING YOUR OWN PERSONALIZED WORK SETTINGS

If you share the use of your computer with others, you may want to keep your own personalized work settings separate from anyone else's. You do this by creating your own User Account. Then, when you log in as a user, you'll see only your own folders, Desktop shortcuts and so on, without having to wade through the folders and documents of other users.

Setting up a new User Account

1. Click on **start** , then on **Control Panel** to open the Control Panel.
2. In the Control Panel, click on **User Accounts** to open the **User Accounts** dialog box.
3. In the **Pick a task...** pane, click on **Create a new account**.
4. Type the name you wish to call the account (e.g. Cheryl), then click on **Next >**.
5. For full access to all functions, click on the **Computer administrator** account type; otherwise click on **Limited**. (To learn about the two account types, in the left panel of the **Pick an account type** window, click on **User account types**.)
6. Click on **Create account** to create the new account.
7. To protect your user account with a password, in the **Pick a task...** pane, click on **Change an account**, then on your **user name**, then follow the prompts.

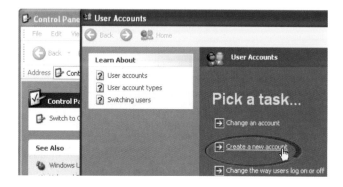
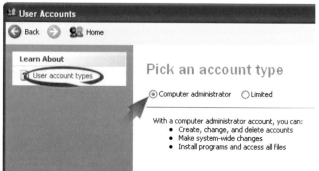

From now on, to start working you'll need to click on your user name to log in to your own settings.

 KEEP YOUR PASSWORD IN A SAFE PLACE
If you decide to create a password, you will have to enter it every time you log in. So write it down in a safe place in case you forget it.

1 Working with spreadsheets (Excel)

Microsoft Office Excel, which comes as part of the Microsoft Office suite of programs, is a popular spreadsheet program that allows you to do a lot of calculations with columns and numbers that would normally be very time-consuming if done with a calculator and a paper spreadsheet. This can be a great advantage for such number-based information as:

- home or business budgets;
- basic accounting;
- sales and profit data and graphic charts;
- price lists;
- invoices;
- statistical analysis, and more.

In addition, you can use Excel to generate professional bar charts, graphs and other graphic representations of your data.

This is all done in what are called spreadsheets, which have the advantage that if you want to change one number – a percentage, a value, or a time-period, and so on – the formulas in the worksheet will automatically recalculate all the other data for you.

So, let's take a look at how Excel works.

STARTING A NEW WORKSHEET IN A NEW WORKBOOK

1. Click on **🏁 start** then **All Programs ▸ Microsoft Office ▸ 🗙 Microsoft Office Excel**, and Excel will open on the Desktop.

Excel will open with a new **workbook** ready for you to start working. Notice (see next page) that the toolbars are in many ways similar to those of Microsoft Office Word. The workbook consists of **worksheets**, each made up of columns and rows that make up the many cells available for inserting information or data. When Excel loads, the cell in the top left corner (Column A, Row 1) has bold borders to indicate that it is selected and ready to have data typed into it.

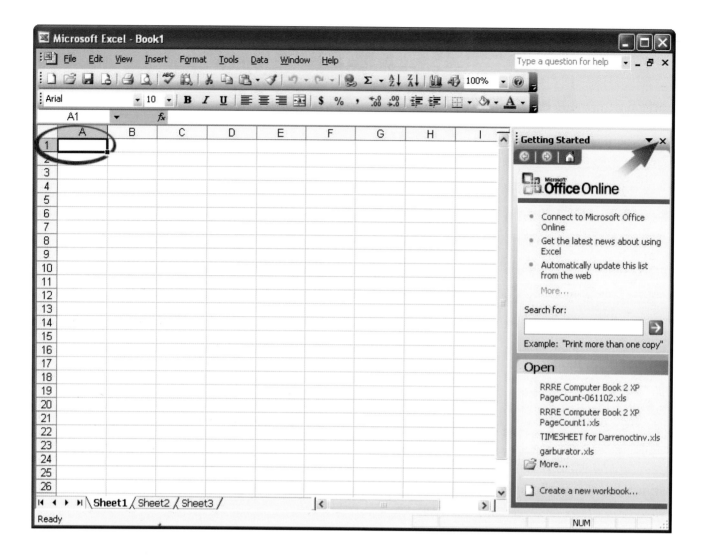

Before you start typing into the worksheet, give the workbook a file name and save it.

2. First, on the **Getting Started** pane on the right, click on the **X Close** button to close the pane. (You can explore this pane later.)

3. Press Ctrl + S and the **Save As** dialog box will open. (By default, the **My Documents folder** should appear in the **Save in:** text window.)

4. In the **File name**: text window type: **MonthlyBudget**.

5. Click on **Save** (or press Enter); the workbook will be saved and its new file name will now appear in the Title Bar at the top.

NAMING A WORKSHEET

Each worksheet within a workbook can be given its own meaningful name on the tabs at the bottom of the sheet.

1. **Right**-click on the tab at the bottom left that says **Sheet1**.
2. In the menu that pops up, click on **Rename**, and **Sheet1** will be selected.
3. Type the word `Expenses` and press `Enter`.

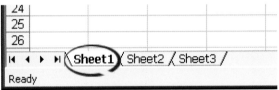

Before renaming

After renaming

NOTE: YOU CAN ADD EXTRA SHEETS

Note that there are additional sheets 2 and 3, and you can add even more sheets to the workbook via the Menu Bar, by clicking on **Insert > Worksheet**.

MOVING THROUGH COLUMNS AND ROWS

	Where you want to go:	**What to do to get there:**
➡	To next cell on the right:	`Tab` key or the `⇨` right arrow key. (Arrow keys only work if the `Num Lock` key is ON.)
⬅	To next cell to the left:	`⇦` left arrow key.
⬇	To next cell down:	`Enter` or `⇩` down arrow key.
⬆	To next cell up:	`⇧` up arrow key.
✛	To any cell:	Click in the cell.
⬅|	To first column, same row:	`Home` key.

ENTERING DATA INTO CELLS

1. If not already selected, click in the first cell **A1** (Column A, Row 1) and type the words: `Our Family Budget`, then press Enter . (Notice how the text extends beyond the border of the cell and that the cell name is also displayed in the cell's Name Box above cell A1.)

2. Click in that first cell (A1) again to select it.

3. Use the formatting toolbar buttons to change the font formatting.

4. Press Enter to give effect to the formatting changes. (The cell selection will jump to the next cell down, cell A2.)

Before Formatting

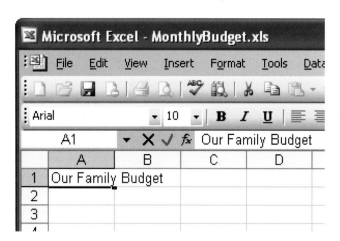

After Formatting

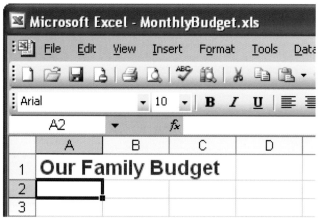

5. Now type the black headings in the cells as shown in the illustration below, using the **B**, **U** and ≣ toolbar buttons to format and centre the headings. (Note: What you type in a cell appears in the formula window above the column headings.)

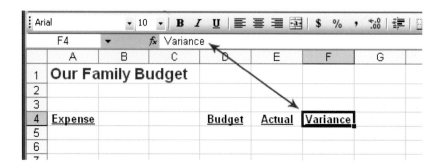

6. Next, select each cell in turn and type in the text and numbers as shown below.

	A	B	C	D	E	F	G
1	Our Family Budget						
2							
3							
4	Expense			Budget	Actual	Variance	
5							
6	Rent			1000	1001		
7	Car			1000	950		
8	School Fees			200	220		
9	Housekeeping			1200	1300		
10	Total						
11							
12							

Now we need to tell Excel what those numbers represent, such as straightforward Numbers, or Currencies, Dates, Percentages, and so on. We first need to select the cells involved so that we can specify the number type for those cells.

SELECTING A RANGE OF CELLS

1. Click in cell **D6** (Column D, Row 6) and **hold down** the mouse button.
2. Now drag the cross-shaped cursor to the right to select **columns D to F**, and down to select **rows 6 to 10**; then release the mouse button; the selected block of cells will now be selected and highlighted.

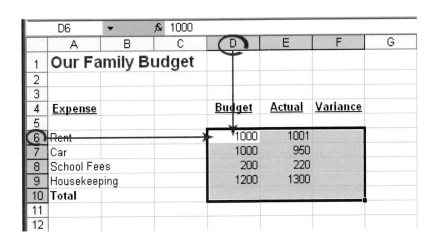

SPECIFYING DATA FORMATS

1. In the Menu Bar, click on **Format > Cells...** and the **Format Cells** dialog box will open at the **Number** tab.

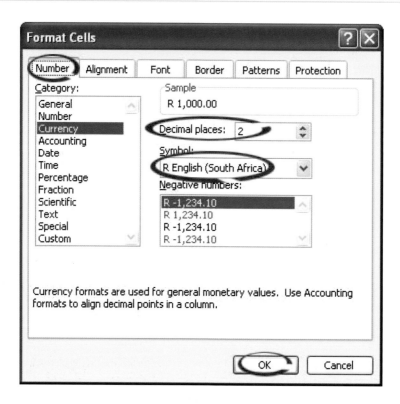

2. Click on **Currency**, then set the **Decimal places:** to **2**, and choose the currency **Symbol:** of your country.
3. Click on **OK**.

TIP: FIXING CELLS WITH ######### IN THEM

If you see a whole lot of these ######### in a cell, it means the column is too narrow to display all the data in it. To fix this, click on the right border in the top shaded bar of that column and, with the mouse button held down, drag the column border a little to the right until all the contents are visible.

	Before expanding column D's width		After expanding column D's width	

	A	B	C	D	E
1	Our Family Budget				
2					
3					
4	Expense			Budget	Actual
5					
6	Rent			########	R 1,001.00
7	Car			########	R 950.00
8	School Fees			R 200.00	R 220.00
9	Housekeeping			########	R 1,300.00
10	Total				

	A	B	C	D	E
1	Our Family Budget				
2					
3					
4	Expense			Budget	Actual
5					
6	Rent			R 1,000.00	R 1,001.00
7	Car			R 1,000.00	R 950.00
8	School Fees			R 200.00	R 220.00
9	Housekeeping			R 1,200.00	R 1,300.00
10	Total				

GETTING EXCEL TO DO YOUR CALCULATIONS FOR YOU

Here comes the fun part. We're going to get Excel to do some calculations for us.

1. Click in cell **D10** to select it.
2. In the **Standard Toolbar**, click on the **Σ AutoSum** button and the formula for automatic additions will appear in the cell and also in the Formula Bar (long window) above.

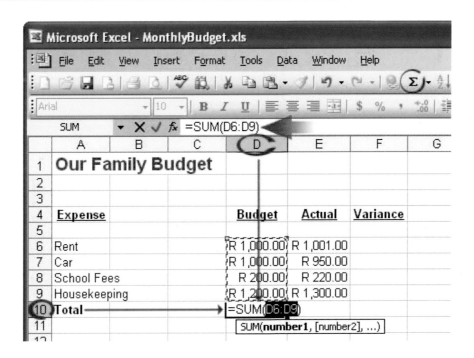

3. Press ⏎ Enter and the selected cell will display the sum of the adjacent numbers above it.

4. Click in cell **E10** and repeat Steps 1 to 3. (Alternatively, click on the little black square Fill Handle on the bottom right corner of cell **D10** (see right) and, while holding the mouse button down, drag the handle across to cell **E10**.)

	D	E
3		
4	**Budget**	**Actual**
5		
6	R 1,000.00	R 1,001.00
7	R 1,000.00	R 950.00
8	R 200.00	R 220.00
9	R 1,200.00	R 1,300.00
10	R 3,400.00	

5. Release the mouse button and the formula will be copied to cell **E10** to give the sum of the numbers above it.

	D	E
3		
4	**Budget**	**Actual**
5		
6	R 1,000.00	R 1,001.00
7	R 1,000.00	R 950.00
8	R 200.00	R 220.00
9	R 1,200.00	R 1,300.00
10	R 3,400.00	R 3,471.00

NOTE: EXCEL ADJUSTS THE FORMULAS

When a formula is copied to another cell, Excel adjusts the formula to make it work for the new column/row.

Now let's see how much the actual expenditure varies from the budget. To do this we need to subtract Column E from Column D, line by line, and in total.

6. Click in cell **F6** to select it.

7. Type an = **(equals)** sign in cell **F6** to tell Excel you wish to start a formula.

8. Click in cell **D6** to select it as the first cell of the formula.

9. Type a – **(minus)** sign to show that you want to subtract a number from the number in cell D6.

10. Click on cell **E6** to select that as the cell you want to subtract.

11. Press ⏎ Enter and the formula will calculate the answer and display in it cell **F6**.

	D	E	F
3			
4	**Budget**	**Actual**	**Variance**
5			
6	R 1,000.00	R 1,001.00	-R 1.00
7	R 1,000.00	R 950.00	
8	R 200.00	R 220.00	
9	R 1,200.00	R 1,300.00	
10	R 3,400.00	R 3,471.00	

COPYING A FORMULA TO OTHER CELLS

Now we need to duplicate the formula for the remaining rows of numbers in column F so that we can get the answers for each line, and also the total.

1. Click in cell **F6** to select it.
2. Click on its **Fill Handle** and drag it downwards to row 10 (cell **F10**) and the formula will now be duplicated for each row, and the answers displayed in each cell.
3. Click anywhere outside the selected area to de-select it.

	D	E	F	G
3				
4	**Budget**	**Actual**	**Variance**	
5				
6	R 1,000.00	R 1,001.00	-R 1.00	
7	R 1,000.00	R 950.00	R 50.00	
8	R 200.00	R 220.00	-R 20.00	
9	R 1,200.00	R 1,300.00	-R 100.00	
10	R 3,400.00	R 3,471.00	-R 71.00	
11				
12				

PROTECTING CELLS CONTAINING FORMULAS

It can be very frustrating to spend a lot of time creating formulas only to lose some of them due to a finger mishap. Therefore, it's best to protect cells that contain formulas. To do this you need to specify which cells you want to be locked, and then protect the whole worksheet in order to protect those locked cells.

By default, if you protect a worksheet all of its cells will be locked and protected. Users will not be able to change the content in any cell until the worksheet itself is unprotected. However, sometimes you want to be able to change data, or add new data, and have Excel use its protected formulas to calculate new results. So you'll need to be able to edit or enter content in some cells while protecting only those with formulas. To protect only certain cells, three steps are required:
1. First unlock all cells in the worksheet (that are already locked by default).
2. Next, select the cells you want to protect, and lock only those cells.
3. Lastly, protect the worksheet itself. The cells that have been locked will now be protected while the unlocked cells can still be edited.

Here is the procedure for doing this.

Stage One: Unlock all the cells

1. In the worksheet, click in the blank shaded area above the Row 1 heading and left of the Column A heading, to select the entire worksheet.
2. On the Menu Bar, click on **Format > Cells... > Protection** tab **> Locked**, to remove the green tick and thereby unlock all the cells.
3. Click on **OK**.

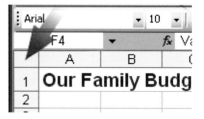

Stage Two: Lock only certain cells (e.g. those containing formulas)

1. Hold down the `Ctrl` key and click in each cell you wish to protect, then release the `Ctrl` key once they've been selected.
2. Follow steps 1, 2 and 3 of Stage One to lock the cells you've selected.

Stage Three: Protect the worksheet to protect the locked cells

1. On the Menu Bar, click on **Tools > Protection ▸ Protect Sheet...** to open the **Protect Sheet** dialog box.
2. In the lower window, click on the first item, **Select locked cells,** to remove the tick so that users won't be able to select or edit those cells.
3. If desired, enter a password in the **Password to unprotect sheet:** text window.
4. Click on **OK**, retype the password and click on **OK** again. (The cells you selected to be locked will now be protected, but users can still access and edit data in other cells.)

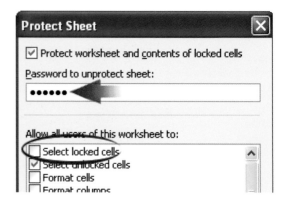

NOTE: YOU CAN ALSO PROTECT EVERY CELL, IF REQUIRED

To protect every cell in the entire worksheet, in the previous step 2, click on the second item too, to uncheck **Select unlocked cells**. This will prevent anyone from accessing any of the cells in the sheet once the sheet has been protected as explained in Stage Three.

NOTE: TO UNLOCK THE PROTECTED CELLS AGAIN

If you later need to amend a formula, click on **Tools > Protection ▸ Unprotect Sheet...**

If you chose to insert a password in step 3 of Stage Three, you will need to enter that password in order to unprotect the sheet.

CREATING CHARTS OF YOUR DATA

Excel will create a professional chart for you from the data you select, and it offers a variety of chart styles from which to choose.

1. Click in cell **A4** and hold down the mouse button while you drag the pointer to the right and downwards until all the cells from **A4** to **F10** are selected.
2. Release the mouse button.

	A	B	C	D	E	F
1	**Our Family Budget**					
2						
3						
4	Expense			Budget	Actual	Variance
5						
6	Rent			R 1,000.00	R 1,001.00	-R 1.00
7	Car			R 1,000.00	R 950.00	R 50.00
8	School Fees			R 200.00	R 220.00	-R 20.00
9	Housekeeping			R 1,200.00	R 1,300.00	-R 100.00
10	Total			R 3,400.00	R 3,471.00	-R 71.00
11						

3. In the Standard Toolbar, click on the 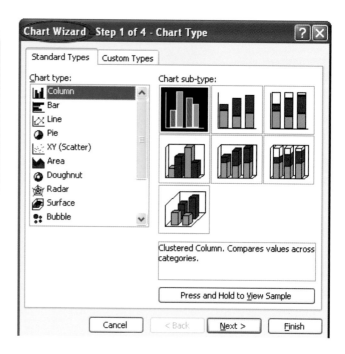 **Chart Wizard** button to open the **Chart Wizard** dialog box at **Step 1 of 4 – Chart Type**.

4. Explore the various options, click on **Next >** and follow the prompts.

USING EXCEL TEMPLATES FOR PROFESSIONAL FORMS

Excel offers templates that can be used for professional forms such as sales invoices, expense statements and time cards. The advantage of using these Excel templates rather than a Word document is that Excel does the calculations for you.

1. On the Excel Menu Bar, click on **File > New...** to open the **New Workbook** panel on the right.

2. Under the **Templates** section, click on the link, **On my computer...** and the **Templates** dialog box will open.

3. Click on the **Spreadsheet Solutions** tab, then click on a form template of your choice.

4. Click on **OK**, and the selected Excel form template will load.

5. Save the file as usual and type into the form the information and data you require; Excel will calculate the totals as necessary.

Creating your own Excel templates

Sometimes the same worksheet design and formulas need to be used repeatedly for different content, and saved under different file names each time. For example:
- a standard job card or quotation to be used for each new job or quote that's done;
- a different price list for each product group, but with the same layout and formulas in each.

Rather than set the whole workbook up again every time you want to start a new job card, quotation or price list, simply create your own reusable template.

To create your own template:
1. Start a new workbook and press `Ctrl` + `S` to save it with a name such as Job Card Design.
2. Create the worksheet that will eventually become your template, and save the final version before saving it as a template per steps 3 to 7.
3. Once you're satisfied that your saved workbook is exactly what you want to use as a template, on the Menu Bar click on **File > Save As...** to open the **Save As** dialog box.
4. In the **File name:** window, type a suitable name, such as Job Card.
5. On the right of the **Save as type:** window, click on the ☑ **down arrow** to open the list of file types.
6. Scroll down and click on **Template (*.xlt)** to select the Template file type.
7. Click on **Save** to save your new template in the Excel Templates folder.

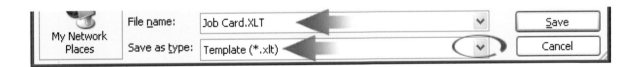

To start a new workbook using your own template:
1. On the Menu Bar, click on **File > New...** to open the **New Workbook** panel on the right.
2. Under the **Templates** section, click on the link, **On my computer...**, and the **Templates** dialog box will open.
3. In the **General** tab, click on **Job Card.xlt** (or whatever file name you gave the new template) to start working in a new workbook. (When you save the workbook it will be saved as a normal workbook (**.xls**) and your template (**.xlt**) file will remain unchanged, ready for future use again.)

OTHER USEFUL EXCEL METHODS

Working in cells

In order to:	You need to do this:
Delete a cell's contents	Click in the cell to select it and press `Del` .
Select a range of adjacent cells	Click in the first cell and drag the mouse cursor over the other cells you want to select.
Move a cell's data content (not a formula) to another cell	1. Click in the cell to select it. 2. Press `Ctrl` + `C` to copy the contents. 3. Click on the destination cell and press `Ctrl` + `V` to paste the copied contents there.
Copy a cell's formula or format	1. Click in the cell and on the Standard Toolbar click on the **Copy** button (or press `Ctrl` + `C`) to copy the source cell's data. 2. Click in the cell you want to copy to. 3. Click on **Edit > Paste Special** and make your selection/s. (The formula copied will be adjusted by Excel to change to the applicable column/row.)
Keep one element of a formula constant	In the Formula Bar, type a **$** sign before the cell column and/or row reference, for example **E4**. (If you copy the formula to another cell, the elements of the formula will be adjusted according to their new column and row – **except** for cell **E4**, which will remain unchanged because of the **$** signs in front of the column/row references.

Using formulas

In order to:	You need to do this:
Add the data in two or more cells	Type a plus (+) sign between the cell references in the Formula Bar, then press Enter ⏎ . For example **=A4+A6+B7**
Multiply the data in two or more cells	Type an asterisk (*) between the cell references in the Formula Bar. For example **=A1*E6** means **A1 x E6**.
Subtract data	Type a minus (–) sign between the cell references, as applicable. For example **=A1–E6** means **E6** will be subtracted from **A1**.
Divide one cell's data by another's	Type a slash (/) before the denominator. For example **=A4/B7** means **A4** will be divided by **B7**.
Express a percentage	Select the cell and click on the ‰ button on the Formatting Toolbar to format the cell as a percentage. On the Toolbar, click on the ⬆ **Increase Decimal** or ⬇ **Decrease Decimal** button as appropriate, to place the decimal point where you need it.
Create a formula using several cells	Place each formula component within brackets. For example **=(B6+C6+D6)*(F8+F9+F10)** (Means: the total of the three cells within the first brackets, multiplied by the total of the three cells in the second brackets.)
Specify a range of cells in a formula	Type a colon between the first and last cell. For example the formula in the item above could be shortened to **=(B6:D6)*(F8:F10)**

Excel offers a wide range of features for working with numbers. These include, for example:
- formatting cells, columns, rows, text and the general appearance of a worksheet;
- linking different worksheets so that if a number on one sheet is changed, Excel will recalculate all the numbers in the linked sheet as well.

TIP: TAKING EXCEL FURTHER

With Excel open, press F1 to display the **Excel Help** pane on the right; click on the Table of Contents link, and explore the various topics.

---

2 Creating slide shows (PowerPoint)

With the Microsoft Office program called PowerPoint you can very easily create your own full-colour, animated slide presentations that can be projected onto a projection screen or viewed by others on their own computers via e-mail or a CD or DVD. Popular uses of slide shows include:

- marketing or financial presentations;
- education and training aids;
- family photo albums, such as holidays, weddings and other celebrations.

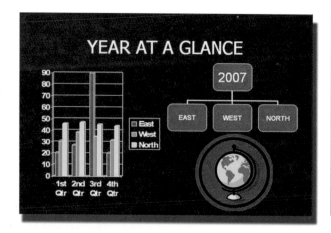

Examples of PowerPoint slides

OPENING POWERPOINT

1. Click on **start** > **All Programs** ‣ **Microsoft Office** ‣ **Microsoft Office PowerPoint**.

PowerPoint will open on the Desktop in Normal View (the bottom left View icon is active) with the **Slides** tab at the top selected. A blank slide will be displayed, ready for you to begin.

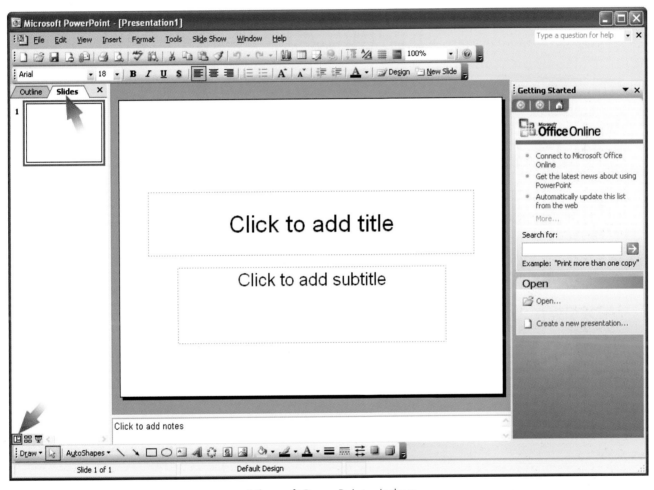

Microsoft PowerPoint window

TIP: SAVE YOUR FILE FIRST

Remember to save your file before you start working on the slide show, to avoid losing a lot of hard work by mistake or through computer failure. Note that, by default, the file will be saved into the My Documents folder in the PowerPoint (**.ppt**) file format. In this format you can create, edit and sort the slides in your presentation.

SHOWING ALL THE TOOLBAR BUTTONS

It's always easier to have all the standard Toolbar buttons visible. However, when there are many of them there's not always enough space for the program to show them all on one Toolbar row. Office programs such as PowerPoint and Word therefore have some of them hidden out of view. You can make them all visible by having them displayed on two rows instead of one.

1. On the far right of the Toolbar, click on the ▪ **Toolbar Options down arrow.**
2. In the little options box that opens showing extra Toolbar icons, click on **Show Buttons on Two Rows**, and those additional icons will now be visible on the Toolbar.

STARTING A NEW PRESENTATION

PowerPoint offers a wide variety of presentation templates, colour schemes and animations, as well as a choice of methods for creating a presentation.

Choosing a method for creating a presentation

There are several ways you can go about creating your presentation, depending on whether you want to be creative or simply follow a series of wizards and fill in the details, letting PowerPoint create the slides for you based on its own templates or content structures. Here are the choices. (More details are given in the pages that follow.)

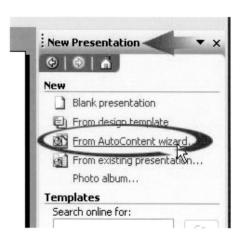

Using the quick and easy AutoContent Wizard:
1. On the Menu Bar, click on **File > New...** and a **New Presentation** pane will open on the right.
2. Click on **From AutoContent wizard...** to open the AutoContent Wizard.
3. Click on **Next >** and follow the prompts to make your choices.

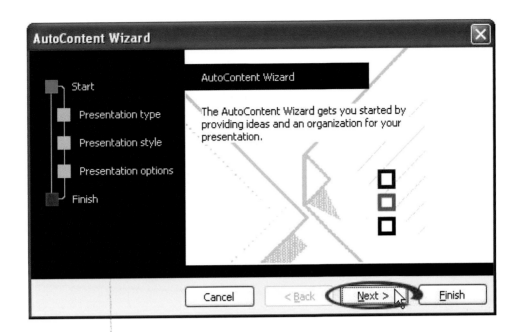

Using one of PowerPoint's many Templates:

1. On the Toolbar, click on the 📝 Design button.
2. In the **Slide Design** pane that opens, click on one of the templates displayed (more step-by-step details are given in the pages that follow).

Designing from scratch:

Use the blank slide that opens when you first load PowerPoint and start typing, with or without the use of the optional PowerPoint templates.

Using the style of a saved presentation:

1. On the **Menu Bar**, click on **File > New...**.
2. In the **New Presentation** pane that opens on the right, click on **From existing presentation...**.
3. In the **New from Existing Presentation** dialog box that opens, browse for the Power-Point file you wish to copy.
4. Click on its file name to select it, and click on the **Create New** button to open a copy of the saved presentation, ready for editing and changing.
5. Click on **File > Save As...** to save the presentation with a different file name.
6. Start editing each slide to create your new presentation content.

CREATING A PRESENTATION

Using PowerPoint's suggested templates

1. On the Formatting Toolbar click on the ⊞ Design button.

The Getting Started pane on the right will be replaced by the Slide Design pane, showing a variety of Design Templates from which to choose.

2. Click on a template's thumbnail image to display a full-size version of the template.
3. Click on the ⌄ scrollbar **down arrow** on the right of the display list to see more template options.
4. To select how you want to apply the design, point to the template of your choice and click on the ⌄ **down arrow** that appears on its right, then click on the menu item you want to apply.

NOTE: TEMPLATES ARE OPTIONAL
If you prefer not to use a template, you can create your own background colours and text layout instead. A template gives an optional overall design scheme within which you can still change the **colour** scheme.

Changing a template's colour scheme

1. In the Slide Design pane, click on **Color Schemes** to select a colour scheme to suit the presentation.
2. Click on the thumbnail image of your choice and your slide will change to the selected colour scheme.
3. Point to the template of your choice again, and click on the down arrow that appears on its right to select how you want to apply the design.

TIP: YOU CAN CHANGE FONT COLOURS
After you've chosen your colour scheme you can still change the template's font colours for words and for lines of text, to suit your needs. Just click on **Edit Color Schemes...**.

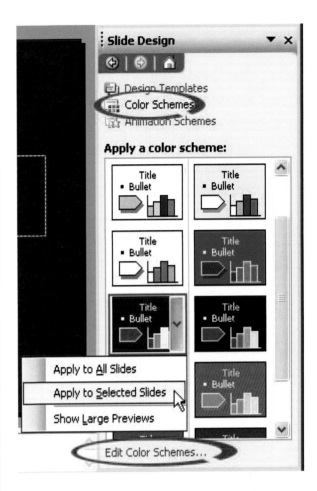

CREATING YOUR OWN BACKGROUND

Choosing a background colour

If you don't want to use any of the templates offered, you can create your own slide show from scratch and give it a background colour and effect of your choice.

1. On the Standard Toolbar click on the  **New** icon to start a new blank presentation.
2. **Right**-click on the slide, and in the menu that opens click on **Background...** to open the **Background** dialog box.

3. Click on the little 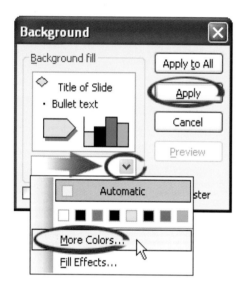 **down arrow** to open the drop-down menu of colours (screenshot below left).

4. Click on **More Colors...** to open the **Colors** dialog box (screenshot below right).

5. Click on the **colour** of your choice, or click on the **Custom** tab to create a custom colour if you need one.

6. Click on **OK** to select your colour and close the **Colors** dialog box, then click on **Apply** to close the **Background** dialog box; the background will change to the colour you selected.

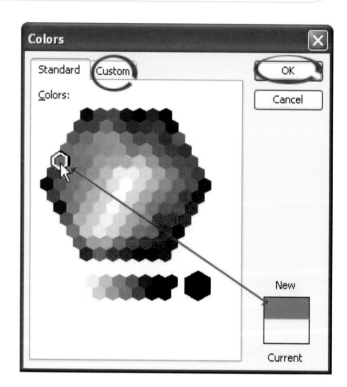

Choosing a background fill effect

1. **Right**-click on the slide, and in the menu that opens click on **Background...** to open the **Background** dialog box.

2. Click on the little 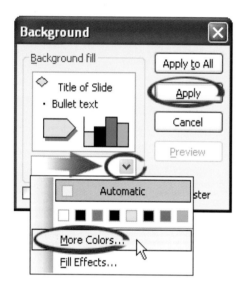 **down arrow** (see screenshot on the left of the next illustration,) to open the drop-down menu of colours.

3. Click on **Fill Effects...** to open the **Fill Effects** dialog box (screenshot on the right).

4. Click on the tabs at the top as well as on the other options below, and explore the various options available.

5. Click on the options of your choice.

6. Under **Variants**, click on each variation to see a sample of the selected option.

7. Click on **OK** to close the **Fill Effects** dialog box, then click on **Apply** to close the **Background** dialog box; the background will change to the colour and effects you selected.

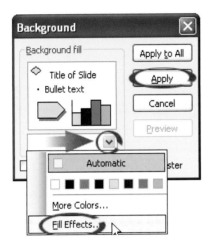

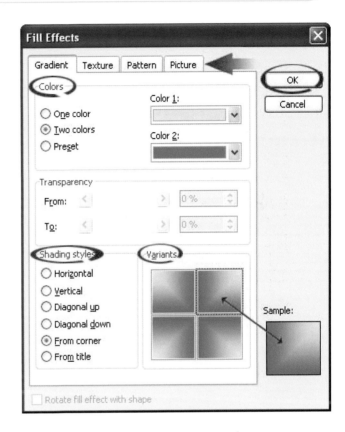

ADDING ELEMENTS TO A SLIDE

To insert a picture:

1. On the Menu Bar, click on **Insert > Picture** ▸, and choose the source (**Clip Art...** or **From File...**).

2. Browse for and click on the Clip Art or picture you want.

3. Click on **OK** and the picture will be inserted into the slide. (It can be repositioned as necessary – see page 30).

To add Text:

1. On the Menu Bar, click on **Insert > Te<u>x</u>t Box** (or click on the 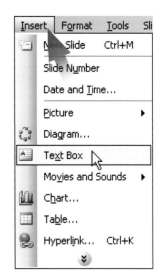 **Text Box** icon on the Drawing Toolbar at the bottom of the PowerPoint window).
2. Type your text into the text box, and format it as required.

DELETING A TEXT BOX OR PICTURE

To delete a Text Box:

1. Click on the text to display the grey Text Box frame.
2. Click on the Text Box **frame** to select the Text Box itself.
3. Press the `Del` key on your keyboard, and the Text Box will be deleted together with all the text it contained.

To delete a picture:

1. Click anywhere on the picture to select it.
2. Press the `Del` key on the keyboard and the picture will disappear.

REPOSITIONING ITEMS

Moving a Text Box to another position

1. Click on the text you wish to move, and the Text Box frame will become visible.
2. Move the mouse pointer to the Text Box **frame** so that the pointer changes to a four-pointed arrow.
3. Click and keep the mouse button depressed.
4. Move the mouse to drag the Text Box to where you want it.
5. Release the mouse button to drop the Text Box into its new position.

Moving a picture

1. Click anywhere in the picture and hold down the mouse button as you drag the picture to where you want it.
2. Release the mouse button to drop the picture into its new position.

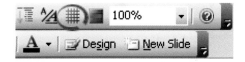

TIP: ALIGNING ITEMS ACCURATELY
To help line things up, click on the **Show/Hide Grid** button on the Toolbar to display gridlines in the slide's background.

Resizing an image, or resizing a Text Box to fit the text

1. Point to any one of the eight resizing **handles** (see little white circles in the Text Box screenshot above) so that the pointer changes to a ↕ **double-pointed resizing arrow**, then click and hold down the mouse button as you drag the handle outwards.
   (The pointer will change to a ✛ crosshair when you click on it.)
2. Release the mouse button.
3. Repeat as necessary with any other handle to obtain the shape and size you need.

TIP: HOW TO RETAIN THE SAME PROPORTIONS
Use the corner handles to retain the height-width proportions while resizing.

1. Click on the text to bring the Text Box frame into view.
2. **Right**-click on the Text Box's grey border, and a menu will open.
3. Click on **Format Text Box...** (sometimes shown as **Format Placeholder...**).
4. In the **Format Text Box** (or **Format Placeholder**) dialog box that opens, click on the tabs at the top to select and change the properties as required.

INDENTING TEXT

You can indent bulleted or unbulleted text to create sub-bullets or subordinate lines of text in a smaller font, or simply create indents with the same font size.

Indenting with a reduction in font size:
1. Click anywhere in the text you want to indent, and a cursor will appear.
2. On the Toolbar, click on the **Increase Indent** button and the text will jump one indent to the right, and the font size will reduce for that item.
3. To create a further indent on the same or the next line, repeat the process.
4. To reduce the indent on any line, click on the **Reduce Indent** button.

Indenting while retaining the same font size:
1. Click on the line of text and press the Home key to take the cursor to the beginning of that line.
2. Press the Tab key once and the text will indent by one tab space.
3. Press the Tab key again and the text will indent by another tab space.
4. To reduce by one tab space, press the BackSpace key once; repeat as necessary.

ADDING ANIMATIONS

You can change the way in which each element of text or image opens on the slide during the slide show. In this way the slide can open with just one line of text, followed later by the next line, next bullet point or an image – with or without sound animations. This is an effective way of keeping the audience's focus where you want it.

1. On the Formatting Toolbar, click on the **Design** button to open the **Slide Design** pane on the right.
2. Click on **Animation Schemes**, and click on each option displayed to see its effect (scroll down to see the full list of available schemes).

SETTING THE TRANSITION FROM ONE SLIDE TO THE NEXT

You can choose how you want each slide to change to the next one (called *slide transition*). You can have a different transition for each slide or use the same transition style for the entire slide show.

1. On the Menu Bar, click on **Slide Show > Slide Transition...** and a list of options will be displayed in the Slide Transition pane that will open on the right.
2. Click on each option to see its effect. (The last option you click on will take effect for that particular slide.)

ADDING A NEW SLIDE TO THE PRESENTATION

On the Toolbar, click on **New Slide** .

TIP: ADD THE SCHEMES AND ANIMATIONS LATER

It's often best to create the entire slide show content first, before doing the animations and slide transitions. In that way you'll have a better idea of what animations and transitions are most appropriate for the presentation as a whole, and for individual slides.

USING THE DIFFERENT VIEW OPTIONS

Slide Sorter View

This is used to sort your slides, copy and paste new slides, and import slides from other presentations. This is accessed via the **View** menu or the icon at the bottom left of the window.

1. On the Menu Bar, click on **View**, then **Slide Sorter** (or click on the **Slide Sorter View** icon at the bottom left of the window).
2. To change the number of slides displayed, on the Toolbar click on the ⌄ **down arrow** to the right of the **Zoom** percentage window.
3. To change the sequence of any slide (or several slides), click on them to select them, then drag them to their new positions. (Alternatively, select the slides and use the Cut and Paste method to move them elsewhere.)

Slide Sorter View

Slide Show View

This allows you to view a full-screen slide show on your computer screen or project it onto a projection screen.

On the Menu Bar, click on **View**, then **Slide Show** (or click on the **Slide Show** icon at the bottom left of the window).

 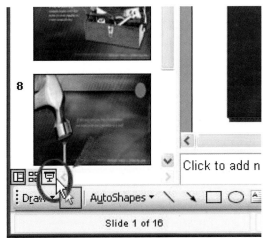

SAVING A PRESENTATION AS A SLIDE SHOW

Once you're satisfied that your presentation is ready for showing as a slide show, you need to save it in the Slide Show **(.pps)** file format (which is different from the default PowerPoint **(.ppt)** format, which is used solely for creating and editing your PowerPoint presentation).

1. On the Menu Bar, click on **File > Save As...** to open the **Save As** dialog box.
2. At the **Save as type:** window, click on the ⌄ **down arrow** on the right to display the list of file types.
3. Click on the scrollbar arrow on the right to scroll down, and click on the **Power-Point Show (*.pps)** file type.
4. Click on **Save** and your presentation will be saved into My Documents (with the same file name but as a **Slide Show** with the **.pps** file extension), ready for presenting.

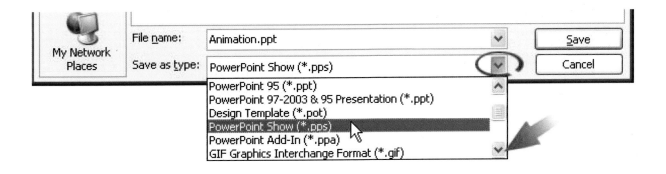

VIEWING A POWERPOINT SLIDE SHOW

1. Open the slide show (**.pps**) file and the first slide will open in full-screen view mode.
2. Click anywhere in the slide to advance to the next slide. (If you used automatic slide transition when you created the presentation, the slides will advance automatically according to the transition timings you had set.)
3. To exit the slide show, press Esc on the keyboard.

LEARNING MORE ABOUT POWERPOINT

Once you've experimented with the procedures covered in this chapter, you can learn more about PowerPoint through its Help pane.

1. On the Toolbar, click on the 🔘 **Microsoft Office PowerPoint Help** button (see screenshot below) to open the **PowerPoint Help** pane.

2. In the Help pane, click on **Table of Contents** (see screenshot below) and explore the many menu items. (Note that some of the links require an Internet connection.)

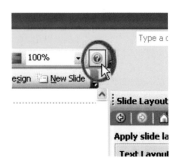

3 More on the Internet and e-mail

Here are some additional useful tips and tricks to get the most out of your time on the Internet – for both e-mail and for the World Wide Web. We'll start with the World Wide Web, which is a major part of the Internet experience.

MAKING INTERNET EXPLORER OPEN AT YOUR FAVOURITE WEB PAGE

Every time you load Internet Explorer it opens at the same Home Page. You can change this default Home Page to be any Web page of your choice – perhaps the daily weather forecast or a site giving the daily news.

1. Open **Internet Explorer**.
2. Connect to the Internet and go to the Web page you'd like to set as your browser's Home Page.
3. On the Menu Bar, click on **Tools**, then on **Internet Options…**.
4. In the **Internet Options** dialog box that opens, click on the **General** tab (see screenshot below right).

5. Just below the **Address:** window, click on the **Use Current** button, and the URL of the Web page you're currently at will automatically appear in the **Address:** window.
6. Click on the **Apply** button, then on **OK**.

ORGANIZING YOUR FAVORITES

You can rearrange your filing system of favorites any time.

To move favorites into different folders:
1. On the Internet Explorer Menu Bar, click on **Favorites > Organize Favorites...** and rearrange your list as you wish.
2. Use the drag-and-drop method to move favorites from one folder to another or to rearrange the sequence of your folders or favorites.

To sort folders and favorites alphabetically:
1. On the Menu Bar, click on **Favorites** to open the list of folders and Web page addresses.
2. **Right**-click anywhere in the **Favorites** list, and in the menu that opens, click on **Sort by Name** to arrange the list in alphabetical order.
3. Repeat step 1, then click on a **Favorites** folder to display its list of Favorites.
4. **Right**-click in that list and, in the menu that opens, click on **Sort by Name** to arrange that folder's Favorites in alphabetical order.

PRINTING A WEB PAGE

Previewing how the page will print

Web pages are designed for viewing on the monitor screen and may print out differently on paper. To avoid wasting paper on pages that don't print the way you expected, it's a good idea to preview the print layout before you click on Print.

1. On the Menu Bar, click on **<u>F</u>ile > Print Preview...** to see how the printed page will look.
2. If you want to change some page settings such as margins, paper size, and so on, click on the 🖼 **Page Setup** button next to the **<u>P</u>rint...** button to open the **Page Setup** dialog box.
3. Make your choices, then click on **OK**.

4. Click on **Close** to return to the normal view.

5. In normal view, press <kbd>Ctrl</kbd> + <kbd>P</kbd> to open the **Print** dialog box, and change any printer settings before you print (e.g. number of copies, print quality), and follow the normal procedure for printing.

Printing a table of the Web page's links

1. Press <kbd>Ctrl</kbd> + <kbd>P</kbd> to open the **Print** dialog box.

2. Click on the **Options** tab and click in the check-box against **Print table of links** to place a green tick in it.

3. Click on the **Print** button at the bottom of the dialog box, and a neat tabulated list of all the links on that Web page will be printed.

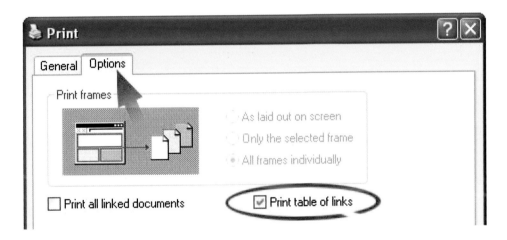

SAVING INK BY NOT PRINTING BACKGROUND COLOURS OR IMAGES

Sometimes you may want to print only the text on the Web page, and not the background colour or Web images. You can specify your requirements in Internet Explorer.

1. On the Menu Bar, click on **Tools > Internet Options...** to open the **Internet Options** dialog box.

2. In the **Internet Options** dialog box, click on the **Advanced** tab and use the scroll bar on the right to scroll down to the **Printing** item.

3. If the **Print background colors and images** item has a tick in its check-box, click on it to remove the tick.

4. Click on **Apply**, then on **OK** and print the page as already explained.

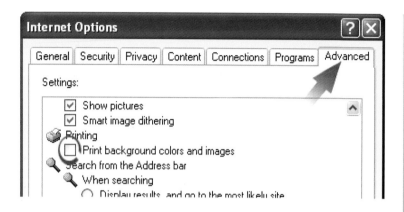

NOTE: WEB SITES WITH A 'PRINT' OPTION ON THEM
Some Web sites have a **Print this page** option (text or button) on the Web page itself. This usually allows printing without background colours and images. To print, simply click on that text link or button.

DOWNLOADING PROGRAMS FROM THE INTERNET

You can download many useful (and often free) programs from Web sites on the Internet and install them very easily onto your system.

TIP: USE THE SAME FOLDER FOR ALL PROGRAM DOWNLOADS
To make things easier for yourself, it's a good idea to save your downloaded program files to the same folder each time so that you can go back to them later if you need to reinstall a program. You can create a folder in My Documents for this purpose and name it, for example, **My Downloads**.

1. Open your browser (e.g. Internet Explorer) and go to this book's companion Web site at **http://www.reallyeasycomputerbooks.com**

2. Once the Web page has loaded, click on **Enter Site**, then on the **Freeware** tab at the top of the page, to access the page with some free programs that can be downloaded.

3. Click on the link **Irfanview** (Photo Editor) to go to the download section for that program, where you can read the download instructions.

4. Click on the link to the Irfanview Web site.

5. At the Irfanview Web site, click on a **Download** link; this will take you to the Web page where the program can be downloaded.

6. At the download page, click on a link that is clearly a link for downloading Irfanview and follow the prompts.

NOTE: DIFFERENT DOWNLOAD SITES

There are many download sites on the Internet. Some program suppliers offer links to several download sites run by independent companies. To make the download as fast and convenient as possible, you can select the download company and the country (sometimes even the city) nearest to you. With experience you will soon get the feel of it.

MINIMIZE VIRUS AND SPYWARE RISKS

To minimize the risk of downloading viruses, spyware or other gremlins onto your system, here are some tips to help you identify trustworthy download sites.

- The program is a well-known and reliable program.
- It can be downloaded at the manufacturer's own Web site, or at a download site linked from the manufacturer's site.
- Tucows and CNet Download are two trustworthy download sites offering a wide range of programs and facilities.

---

7. When the **File Download – Security Warning** dialog box opens, click on the **Save** option to download and save the executable (**.exe**) file to your computer.

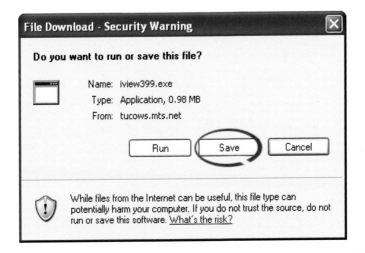

8. In the **Save As** dialog box that opens, click on the ![down arrow icon] **down arrow** at the right of the **Save in:** window to select the destination folder to which you'd like to save the file (e.g. **My Downloads**).

9. If the destination folder is visible in the main pane, **double**-click on it to bring it up into the **Save in:** window. (The lower **Open** button will change its name to **Save**.)

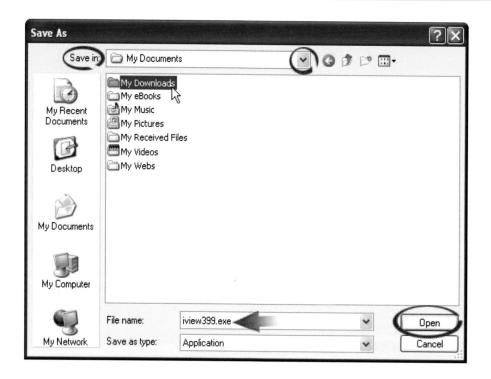

10. Make a written note of the file name shown in the **File name:** window so that you'll recognize it when you go to the destination folder later to install the program.

11. Click on **Save** to commence the download process.

A window will pop up to tell you when the download has been completed.

12. To start the installation immediately, click on **Run**.

13. To install the program later (see next topic), click on the **Close** button. (If you have a tick against the **Close this dialog box when download completes**, the dialog box will close automatically.)

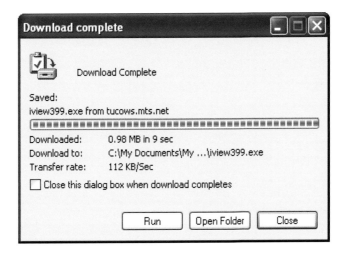

INSTALLING A DOWNLOADED PROGRAM

The usual installing procedure

1. Use **Windows Explorer** or **My Computer** to locate the downloaded file in the folder to which it was saved, and **double**-click on it to open it.
2. If a **Security Warning** box opens, click on **Run** (because this particular program is safe to run), then follow the prompts as the various installation dialog boxes come up.

ADDITIONAL DOWNLOAD ADVICE
Don't download any programs without having an up-to-date anti-virus program installed, and your Windows Firewall enabled. (Refer to Book 1 (XP) for more details.)

Also, some people get carried away with the idea that they can obtain free programs from the Internet, so they download will-nilly and end up with a system that slows down because of all the unnecessary programs they've installed. If you're not using a program frequently, then uninstall it rather than have an inefficient and slow system.

More on E-mail with Outlook Express

CREATING EXTRA MAIL FOLDERS

It can sometimes be useful to file your e-mails into separate folders – for example: Family, Club, Customers, and so on. We recommend, however, that you limit the number of additional folders to what is really essential; otherwise you can create a new problem of remembering into which folder a particular e-mail was filed.

1. On the Outlook Express Menu Bar, click on **File > New ▸ Folder...** to open the **Create Folder** dialog box.
2. In the **Folder name:** text window type the name you wish to give your new folder (e.g. Family).
3. In the lower pane, click on the folder into which you want to place the new folder. (**Local Folders** is normally a good place to have additional folders stored.)
4. Click on **OK**.

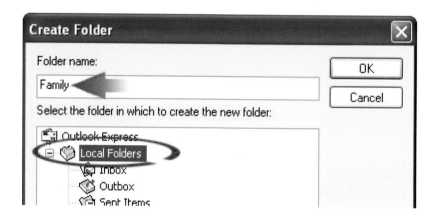

You can now move relevant incoming and outgoing mail from the standard folders to your customized folders. Alternatively, you can tell Outlook Express to do that for you automatically when an e-mail is sent or received, according to specific rules you have set up (see next main topic).

Renaming, moving or deleting a folder

1. In the list of folders in Outlook Express, click on the folder you wish to select.
2. On the Menu Bar, click on **File > Folder**, then on **Rename...**, **Move...** or **Delete...**, as required.

SETTING RULES FOR AUTOMATIC MAIL HANDLING

With Message Rules, you can tell Outlook Express how to handle mail to or from a particular sender, or where the Subject line contains certain text, and so on. Based on the rules you set, such mail can be sent immediately to a specified folder, or deleted, forwarded, removed from the mail server at your ISP (Internet Service Provider) without being downloaded to your computer, and so on. This can be very useful in helping to reduce the amount of organizing you need to do manually, especially if you have quite a lot of e-mail movement each day.

1. On the Menu Bar, click on **Tools > Message Rules ▸ Mail...** to open the **New Mail Rule** dialog box. (If the **Message Rules** box opens first (see screenshot below), click on the **Mail Rules** tab, then on **New...**, to open the **New Mail Rule** dialog box.)

2. In the **New Mail Rule** dialog box, scroll through the list of **Conditions** in pane number 1 and select at least one, but more if you wish.
3. Do the same for the **Actions** in pane number 2. (As each item is checked, a hyperlink will appear in the last pane.)
4. Next, in pane number 3, click on each underlined hyperlink to open the **Type Specific Words** dialog box.

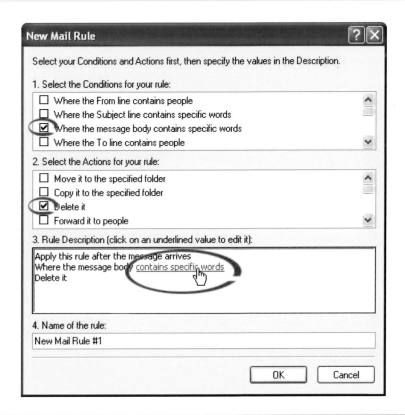

5. In the **Type Specific Words** dialog box, type the specific conditions or actions for your rule. (This will be for this particular rule only. You can add more new rules using this same procedure.)

6. Click on **Add** to return to the **New Mail Rule** dialog box.

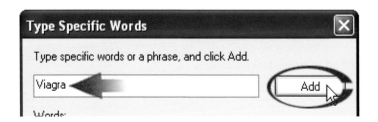

7. Lastly, in pane number 4 enter a brief description of this rule, or simply accept what's offered by Outlook Express.

8. Click on **OK** and your rule will apply to future incoming or outgoing e-mails affected by this rule.

USING SIGNATURES IN OUTGOING MAIL

A **signature** is simply a pre-typed piece of text that can be added automatically at the end of your outgoing e-mail letters. You can create several signatures: one for your personal use, another for your business, yet a different one for your sports club, and so on. You can also format the signatures as you wish.

1. On the Outlook Express main Menu Bar, click on **Tools > Options...**.

2. In the **Options** dialog box that opens, click on the **Signatures** tab.

3. Click on the **New** button.

4. In the **Edit Signature** pane, type the signature you want to use.

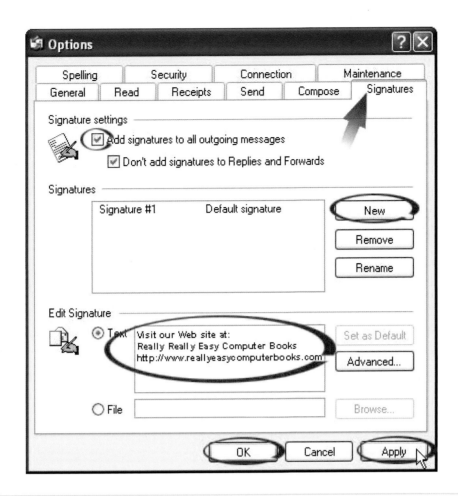

5. To have the signature appear on all outgoing e-mails, click the check-box next to **Add signatures to all outgoing messages**.

6. Click on **Apply**, then on **OK**.

You can create several different signatures in this way (see next topic).

SENDING E-MAIL FROM DIFFERENT NAMES (ACCOUNTS)

You can set up additional 'accounts' or 'personalities' so that the name that appears in the **From** line in e-mails that you send will be according to the personality (account) you chose when you created the new message. You can also decide which signature will be matched to each sender account so that the correct signature will always be included automatically. This is also handy if more than one person in a household is using the same computer.

To set up additional e-mail accounts you'll need your Internet connection and e-mail account log-in and server details at hand, because you will need them for this procedure.

Finding your e-mail log-in details

1. In Outlook Express, click on **Tools**, then on **Accounts...** to open the **Internet Accounts** dialog box.

2. Click on the **Mail** tab, then on the **Properties** button and the **Account Properties** dialog box will open.

3. From the **General** tab make a note of the details shown.

4. Click on the **Servers** tab and make a note of the **Incoming mail (POP3):** and **Outgoing mail (SMTP):** mail servers and the login name in the **Account name:** window.

5. Click on **Cancel** to close the **Account Properties** dialog box.

6. Keep the **Internet Accounts** dialog box open for the next steps.

Creating your new account

7. Next, click on the **Add** ▸ button, then on **Mail...** to add a new Mail account.

8. In the **Your Name** dialog box that opens first, type the name that you want others to see when they receive e-mails from this account, for example: **Really Easy Computer Books**.

9. Next, follow the prompts in the **Internet Connection Wizard** and fill in the relevant details you've already noted in steps 3 and 4 above.

10. When done, click on **Finish**.

Sending an e-mail from your alternative account

1. Start a new mail message as usual.
2. At the far right edge of the **From:** window, click on the ✔ **drop-down arrow button.**
3. Click on the account from which you want to send your e-mail, and it will appear in the **From:** window.
4. Complete your e-mail and send it.

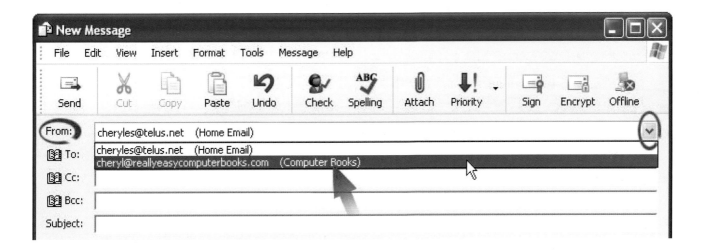

SENDING TO A GROUP OF PEOPLE USING ONE ADDRESS BOOK ENTRY

If you have a group of people to whom you regularly need to send an e-mail – members of a club, for example – you can create one Group entry in your address book that contains all their e-mail addresses. To address your e-mail you then need select only the group name, and everyone in that group will receive the e-mail. If you have several such groups, you can set up several Group entries in your address book. Recipients can appear in more than one group.

> **NOTE: SHOW THE Bcc ICON**
>
> For the next procedure, open a New Message window and make sure that the 🕮 Bcc: button is showing above the **Subject:** line. If not, in the Menu Bar click on **View**, then on **All Headers**.

1. On the main Outlook Express Toolbar, click on the **Addresses** button to open the **Address Book – Main Identity** window.
2. On the **Address Book – Main Identity** toolbar, click on the 🖾 **New** button and then click on **New Group...** to open the **Properties** dialog box at the **Group** tab.
3. In the **Group Name:** text window type the name of your new group.

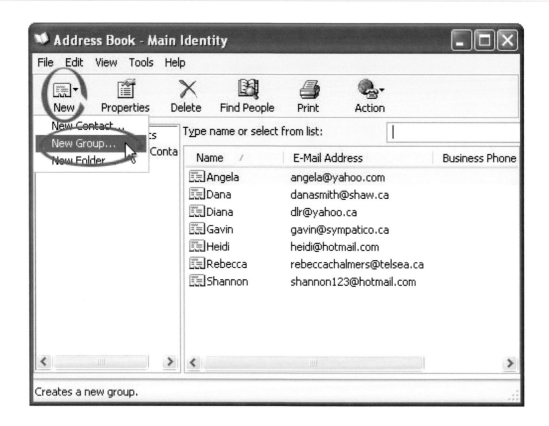

Adding existing contacts:
1. To select recipients from your Address Book, click on the **Select Members** button to open up the list of contacts.
2. Next, hold down the Ctrl key and click on each contact you wish to add to the group. (Scroll down if necessary, to see more contacts.)
3. When done, click on the **Select - >** button, then on **OK**.

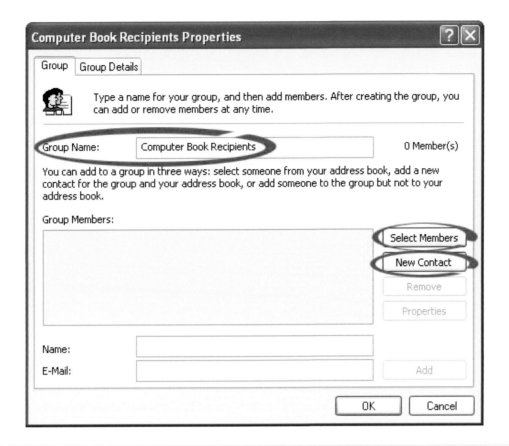

Adding new contacts:

1. If you wish to add a new contact not already in your Address Book, click on the **New Contact** button (see screenshot above).

2. In the **Properties** dialog box that opens, type the details of your new contact, then click on **Add**, then on **OK**, and the contact will be added to the group.

Viewing a list of your groups

1. In the Address Book Menu Bar, click on **View**.

2. If there is no tick against the item **Folders and Groups**, click on it to select it.

TIP: HIDING THE NAMES OF GROUP MEMBERS

When you send an e-mail to the Group address, the e-mail addresses of all the group members are displayed in the e-mail when it is received by each recipient. Therefore, to protect the privacy of all recipients, remember to place the group entry in the **Bcc:** window of your e-mail.

---

4 Introducing other programs

TIME-MANAGEMENT WITH MICROSOFT OUTLOOK

Microsoft Outlook (the senior version of Outlook Express) is essentially a personal organizer – an e-mail program, diary, scheduler, reminder system, scribble pad, and more. You can arrange the views and options to suit your own needs, and set alarms to remind you of important tasks and diary events. If you like to be highly organized, you'll find Outlook a very useful support tool.

Outlook is so versatile, with so many options, that we'll simply introduce you to the program and invite you to explore the many Toolbar icons and menus at your leisure.

Starting Outlook

1. Click on **start** > **All Programs** ▸ **Microsoft Office** ▸ **Microsoft Office Outlook**, and Outlook will open on the Desktop.

2. In the **Outlook Shortcuts** panel at the bottom left of the main Outlook window, click on each item in turn to see what it offers.

3. To explore each item's options, click on the various **Menu** and **Toolbar** items at the top.

4. Note also the little **Notes** icon below the four larger buttons at the bottom.

Calendar View by Month

1. On the Toolbar, click on the **Microsoft Office Outlook Help** button to open the **Outlook Help** pane.
2. Click on **Table of Contents** and explore the many menu items. (Note that some of the links require an Internet connection.)

PROTECTING IMPORTANT FILES WITH WINDOWS BACKUP

BACKING UP IS CRUCIAL

If you have a lot of files stored on your computer – representing a lot of important information or hard work – the last thing you want is to lose them all as a result of program corruption or a computer 'crash', where the hard drive becomes unusable and data gets corrupted.

It is therefore critically important to save your important files to some storage device other than your computer, so that if you do have hardware or software problems, and you lose the data on your hard drive, you have another storage place where you've kept a backup copy safe and sound. Windows Backup is the program that enables you to backup your files.

How often you do a backup depends on how often you add or update files. Some people need to do a daily backup, others backup once a week.

There are several ways in which you can keep a backup of your important files, and different 'experts' will recommend different 'best' methods. You can do a one-time backup of all your data files and then do regular backups of the files that have changed or been added since your first complete backup.

NOTE: STORAGE DEVICES FOR BACKUPS

There are various options for storing your backup files, depending on how large your total backup will be and therefore how much storage capacity you will need.

Rewritable CDs or DVDs: CDs have a capacity of around 700 megabytes, DVDs about 4.7 gigabytes (i.e. much more). Both are stable and therefore safe storage devices. You'll need a CD or DVD Writer either installed on your computer or as an external piece of hardware. You'll also need a supply of rewritable disks that can be used over and over.

A second hard drive (a very good option): This can either be one that's installed on your computer, or a separate hard drive that can be connected to your computer via a USB cable.

1. Click on **start** > **All Programs** ‣ **Accessories** ‣ **System Tools** ‣ **Backup** to open the **Backup or Restore Wizard**. (It's a good idea to create a Desktop shortcut to this important facility – see next chapter for the procedure.)

2. Click on **Next >**, and in the **Backup or Restore** dialog box that opens click on **Backup files and settings**, then click again on **Next >**.

3. In the **What to Back Up** dialog box that opens, click on the item you wish to backup (usually the first item, **My Documents and settings**), and click on **Next >**.

4. In the **Backup Type, Destination, and Name** box that opens, click on the **Browse...** button to open the **Save As** dialog box; select the drive to which you'll save the files.

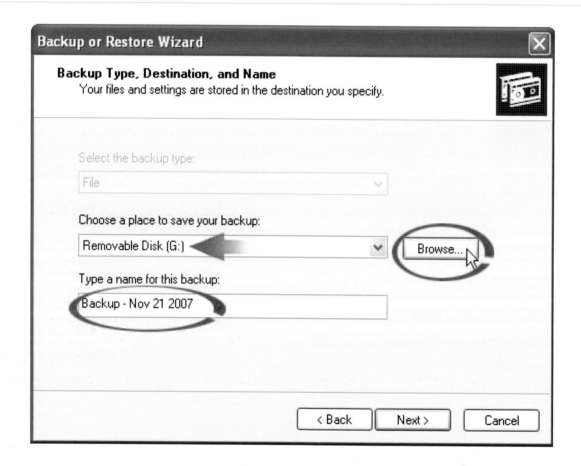

Saving to a rewritable disk

1. Insert a blank CD or DVD disk into the CD/DVD drive.
2. To choose the destination drive (previous step 4), in the **Save As** dialog box click on the ⬆ **Up One Level** green arrow until **My Computer** is visible in the main window.
3. **Double**-click on **My Computer** to bring it up to the **Save in:** window.
4. In the main window, **double**-click on the **CD** or **DVD/CD** drive to bring it up into the **Save in:** window; you're now ready to start the backing up process.
5. Click on **Finish**.

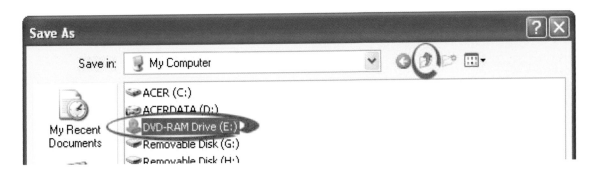

A backup progress window will open showing the progress and the estimated remaining time for the backup to be completed.

Restoring backup files after a system crash

Hard drives can fail at any time, usually without warning. When this happens you'll need to have your computer fixed, which will possibly require a new hard drive to be installed, in which case you'd probably lose all your data files in the process. However, if you have been vigilant about doing regular and frequent backups, you can restore all the files from your backup disk onto your new hard drive.

Follow the same procedure as for backing up files, but in step 2 in the backing-up steps click on **Restore files and settings** instead of on the backup option.

EXPLORING THE ACCESSORIES APPLICATIONS

There are some other nifty applications that can be explored via the Accessories menu.

1. Click on **⟨⟨ start⟩⟩** > **All Programs** ▸ **Accessories** to view the various applications available.
2. Where a menu item shows an arrowhead ▸ , click on the item to expand the menu.

TIP: BE WILLING TO EXPLORE

Programs are there to be used, so be prepared to explore what's available and to click on the menu items and toolbar icons to get a feel of a program's potential for your own situation, and also to learn how it functions. When you're done exploring one program, click on **Cancel** or **Close** before opening and exploring the next.

EXPLORING OTHER APPLICATIONS FROM THE START MENU

Click on **⟨⟨ start⟩⟩** > **All Programs** to see what other applications can be accessed. (Three of these are mentioned below.)

Games: Bored? Click on **Games** and enjoy the challenges of some of the computer games available with Windows XP.

Remote assistance: If you have a problem and need the help of a trusted friend or family member at a different location, you can give them permission to access your computer via the network or an Internet connection, provided you're both using the Windows XP operating system.

Windows Messenger: Windows Messenger allows you to communicate 'live' with someone else who is connected to the Internet at the same time as you are. You'll be able to see which of your contacts are online, exchange text communications and ask for remote assistance from a friend who's online. Windows Messenger also integrates with Outlook Express, where your Messenger Contacts can be displayed in your Contact folder.

The next chapter gives some useful tips on how to work with programs and windows.

5 Working with programs and windows

The system that makes your computer function in response to the commands you give it is called the Operating System. This book is based on the Windows XP operating system.

The *software* you use to tell the computer to do certain things is comprised of *programs* (or *applications* as they are often referred to). There are programs for writing documents, sending and receiving electronic mail (e-mail), viewing Web sites on the Internet, viewing and editing pictures, listening to music, doing accounting, playing games, and more. A program appears on your screen as a *window*.

This chapter is about opening, closing and working with programs and their windows and dialog boxes.

LOADING A PROGRAM QUICKLY FROM A SHORTCUT

A quick way to open any program – for example, Microsoft Office Word – is to do so from a shortcut icon, either on the Desktop or, better still, from the Quick Launch Toolbar.

Creating a shortcut on the Desktop

1. Click on **start** and the Start Menu will pop up.
2. Point to **All Programs** to open the All Programs sub-menu.
3. Find the program called **W Microsoft Office Word** and **right**-click on it. (The sequence would usually be **All Programs ▸ Microsoft Office ▸ Microsoft Office Word**.)

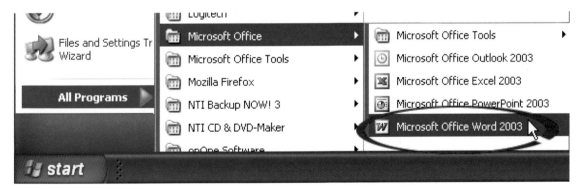

Start Menu cascade

4. In the overlaying sub-menu that opens, click on **Send To ▸ Desktop (create shortcut)**.

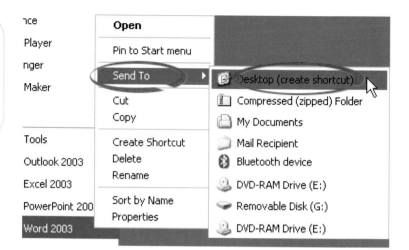

An icon will appear on your Desktop with a small curved arrow to indicate that it's a shortcut. To open Word from the Desktop shortcut, simply double-click on the icon. With this method you'll no longer need to wade through the Start menu every time you want to load Word.

Desktop Shortcut to Word

USING THE QUICK LAUNCH TOOLBAR

If you have several programs open it's often quicker to open a new program from a shortcut icon on the Quick Launch Toolbar (see below) because, unlike the Desktop, this toolbar is always in view.

Icons on the Quick Launch Toolbar to the right of the Start button

If no icons are displayed there, you can make the Quick Launch Toolbar visible as follows:

1. **Right**-click on a blank area of the **Taskbar** (the blue strip to the right of the start button).

2. In the menu that pops up, point to **Toolbars**, and in the new sub-menu that opens, click on **Quick Launch**.

Placing a copy of a Desktop shortcut on the Quick Launch Toolbar

1. On the Desktop, click on the **Microsoft Office Word** shortcut icon and keep the mouse button depressed while you move the mouse towards you to drag the pointer (and the icon) down onto the **Quick Launch Toolbar**.
2. When the pointer is on the Quick Launch Toolbar a vertical black line will indicate where the icon will be positioned when you release the mouse button.

3. Release the mouse button and your shortcut to **Word** will now appear on the **Quick Launch Toolbar**. (It will remain on the Desktop as well.)

TIP: MANY ICONS ON THE QUICK LAUNCH TOOLBAR
If you want to have many shortcut icons on the Quick Launch Toolbar, it's best to click on its dotted vertical line and drag it off the Taskbar to the side or the top of the screen. Then, to change the toolbar's properties, right click anywhere on its grey area to open a menu of options.

Deleting a shortcut

1. On the Desktop, or the Quick Launch Toolbar, click once on the shortcut icon you want to delete, and press Del .
2. In the confirmation box that pops up click on **OK**, and the shortcut will disappear from either the Desktop or the Toolbar, depending on which icon you deleted.

WINDOW CLOSING OPTIONS

Here are the four most common ways to close a window.

Method 1	Method 2	Method 3	Method 4
With the window open and active, click on the ☒ **Close** button at the top right corner of the active window.	With the window open and active, press Alt + F4 .	Right-click on the window's task icon on the Taskbar, then click on the **Close** menu option.	With the window open and active, on the Menu Bar click on **File**, then on **E<u>x</u>it**.

TIP: WORKING IN SEVERAL WINDOWS

When two or more programs or files are loaded, if their windows are maximized, only one will be visible on the Desktop, but they will all have their task icons located on the Taskbar. The window that is visible on the screen will have its Taskbar icon 'depressed' and darker to show that it is the active window. If you click on the Taskbar button of a non-active window, that window will appear on the screen over the one that was previously visible. This is useful when you need to work in more than one program and switch back and forth between them. You simply click on the Taskbar button of the window you wish to view.

MINIMIZING ALL PROGRAMS AT ONCE, WITH ONE CLICK

If you have several programs running (i.e. you're 'multi-tasking'), you can use the Show Desktop shortcut button to view your Desktop with just one click, without having to minimize each program one by one to send them to the Taskbar.

Open several programs and/or documents, one after the other — e.g. **Word**, **Internet Explorer**, **Outlook Express**, and whatever other programs or files you want to load, so that your Desktop is obscured and there are several program/file buttons on the Taskbar.

Now try these two methods to get to the Desktop.

The long method:

1. Click on the **Minimize** button of the window that is filling your screen to send it to the Taskbar.
2. Repeat this to minimize the next window that is filling the screen.
3. Do it repeatedly until the Desktop is in view.

Restore the programs again:

1. Click on each task button on the Taskbar in turn to restore each of those windows to the screen again. (They will be one behind the other. This will bring you back to where you were before using the long method.)

The one-click method:

1. On the **Quick Launch Toolbar**, click once on the **Show Desktop** icon; all the programs will be sent to the Taskbar and your Desktop will be in full view.

RESIZING A WINDOW

You can move a window (or a dialog box) around on your screen, and you can make a window (not a dialog box) wider or taller. This is very useful when you want to move one window out of the way to see something it's obscuring (such as a Help window), but without closing the window altogether.

NOTE: ONLY WINDOWS NOT MAXIMIZED CAN BE RESIZED OR MOVED

Resizing and moving windows works only when the window is **not** in the maximized size, i.e. only when the **maximize** button is visible in the top right corner. Note too that only the window that has the dark border at the top is the active window. Windows with a light border are inactive and won't respond until you click somewhere within that window or on the top title bar to reactivate the window. Note too that dialog boxes cannot be maximized or resized.

Making a window wider

1. With any window open (for example Word), click once on the little 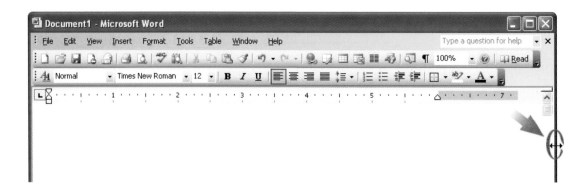 **Restore** button at the top right of the window. The window will normally shrink in size.
2. Now slowly and carefully move your mouse so that the pointer hovers over the right-hand border of that window.
3. Move it ever so slightly and slowly until the pointer changes its shape to a small double-headed resizing arrow (you may have to move it just a fraction to the left or right until it changes shape), then stop and hold it there.

4. With the pointer in that double-arrow shape, click and hold down the mouse button.
5. Now, drag the border a little to the left or right, and notice how the window gets narrower or wider, according to the direction in which you dragged.
6. Release the mouse button and the window will stay at that new size.

You can do this on any border, and even on a corner.

Maintaining the proportion while resizing

1. Position the pointer on the **top left corner** of the window until it changes shape to a 45-degree-angled double-arrow line.

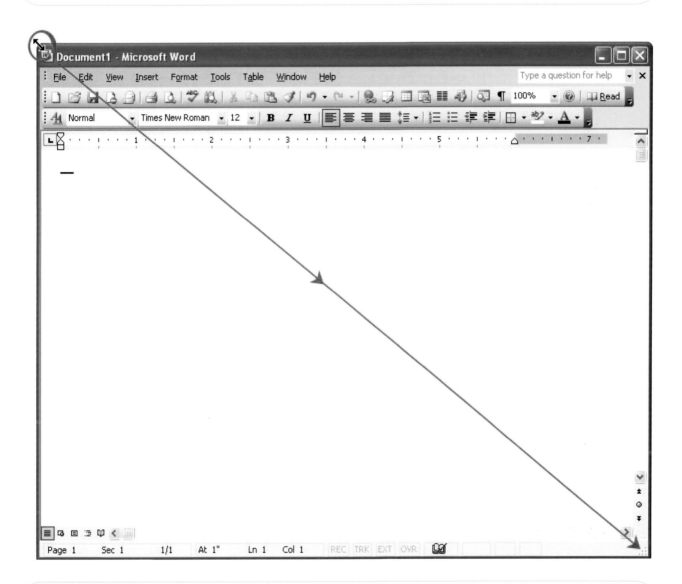

2. Click and hold down the left mouse button.
3. Now slowly drag the little black resizing arrows down **towards the bottom right corner** of that window, and see how it shrinks the whole window proportionately.
4. Release the button.
5. Now do that again but drag the corner **outwards** so that the window becomes larger again. (Try doing this from other corners and sides too.)

MOVING A WINDOW'S POSITION ON THE SCREEN

Here's how to move a window to another position on your screen, without changing its size.

1. With the window in Restore size (not maximized), make sure it's resized to about half the screen size; if not, resize it as just explained.
2. Click in the **blue border** at the top of that window and hold down the mouse button. (Your display settings may show the border as some colour other than blue, but the process is the same.)
3. Now carefully drag the pointer upwards and then let go. The whole window will move up accordingly.
4. Now click again in the blue border and hold down the mouse button.
5. Drag the pointer to the left, and the whole window will move to the left.
6. Now click on the ◼ **Maximize** button on the top right of that window to maximize the window back to its full size to fill your screen.

You can do this with almost any program's window to enable you to view several windows at the same time. This can be useful when you're reading instructions in one window, like a Help menu, and doing the suggested task in the main window: just drag the Help window out of the way. Or, if you are working in Word and researching information on the Internet at the same time, you can have both your Word program and your browser open at the same time and have each one reduced to fill one half of the screen, either side by side or one above the other.

Displaying several windows side by side

1. **Right**-click on a blank area of the Taskbar to display a menu (see right).
2. Click on **Tile Windows Vertically** to show all the open windows alongside one another.

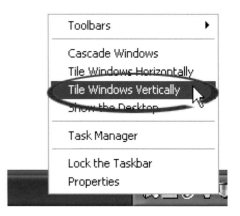

> **TIP: DISPLAYING WINDOWS ONE ABOVE THE OTHER**
> Follow the same procedure as described above, but click on **Tile Windows Horizontally**. To revert to the normal display, right-click on the Taskbar again, and click on **Undo Tile**.

ARRANGING SHORTCUT ICONS THE WAY YOU WANT THEM

If you have a fair number of shortcut icons on your Desktop, it's often useful to rearrange them in groups so that you can find them easily. For example, you could have all your Internet icons grouped together (Internet Explorer, Outlook Express, Windows Messenger, and so on), and your document programs and multimedia programs in their own groups.

Moving shortcut icons on the Desktop using drag-and-drop

1. **Right**-click on any blank area of the **Desktop**.
2. In the menu that pops up, point to **Arrange Icons By ▸** and make sure that **Auto Arrange** has **no** tick next to it. If it has a tick, click on **Auto Arrange** to remove the tick and enable you to move the Desktop icons yourself. The menu will close.

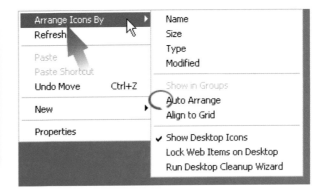

3. Back on the Desktop, click on any shortcut icon and **hold down** the mouse button.
4. Move the mouse pointer and the icon will move with it. This is called **dragging**.
5. **Release** the mouse button and the shortcut icon will stay where you 'dropped' it.
6. Repeat the procedure with any other shortcut icons.

Lining up icons neatly on the Desktop

To line up the icons neatly:
1. **Right**-click on the Desktop, then click on **Arrange Icons By**.
2. In the sub-menu that pops up click on **Align to Grid** and a tick will appear next to it to show it has been selected, so that in their new positions all the icons will be aligned in their respective rows. They will remain in the columns in which you dropped them.

To arrange the icons in sequence of name, size, type, or date modified:
1. **Right**-click on the Desktop, then click on **Arrange Icons By**.
2. In the sub-menu that pops up, click on the option of your choice.

Changing the order of icons on the Quick Launch Toolbar

1. Click on the icon you wish to move and hold down the mouse button.
2. Drag the icon along the Quick Launch Toolbar to where you want it.
3. When the short solid black line across the toolbar is at the desired position, release the mouse button and the icon will drop into its new position.

REMOVING INSTALLED PROGRAMS

When you no longer need a program that you've installed, remove it from your system. You can always reinstall it again at a later date if you change your mind. To do this you don't simply delete it; you need to go through the proper uninstall procedure.

WHEN INSTALLING OR UNINSTALLING

When installing or uninstalling programs (software) or equipment (hardware), it is important to do the following:

1. **Beforehand:** Always save your current work, then close all programs before installing or uninstalling programs.
2. **Afterwards:** Always restart your computer when the installing or uninstalling has been completed.

1. Click on **start** > **Control Panel**.
2. **Double-click** on the **Add or Remove Programs** item to open the **Add or Remove Programs** dialog box.
3. At the top left of the window, click on the button **Change or Remove Programs** (see red arrow in the next screenshot) to select it.
4. If the **Show updates** check-box isn't ticked, click on it so that an updated list of programs is always displayed in the Add or Remove Programs dialog box.
5. In the list of programs in the main window, click on the program you want to uninstall.
6. Click on the **Change/Remove** button and follow the prompts. (Some programs can't be changed, only removed, in which case you will see a **Remove** button.)

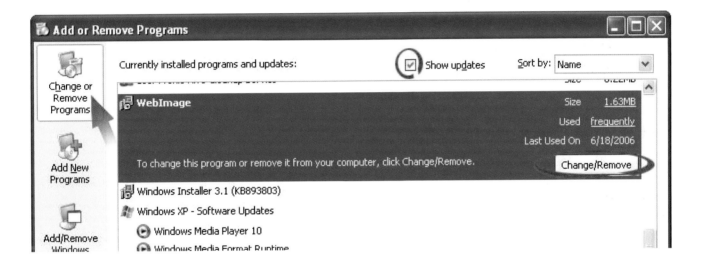

6 Managing folders and files

Anyone who stores items of some kind or another – documents, photos, etc. – at home or at work will know that if you don't have an efficient method of storage you can waste a lot of time hunting for things. The same applies to what's stored on a computer.

NOTE: FOLDERS AND FILES EXPLAINED

A **file** is a collection of digital data stored in a particular format according to the nature of the data. The file name is followed by a dot and an extension to the name to indicate the format of the data, e.g. a document (**.doc**), a worksheet (**.xls**), an image (**.jpg** or **.gif**), a sound (**.wav**).

A **folder** is a place in which files may be stored. It is represented on the screen by an icon that looks like a typical manila filing folder used to store documents in a filing cabinet. A folder may also contain other folders, often called sub-folders.

MANAGING FOLDERS AND FILES WITH WINDOWS EXPLORER

The program we'll be using in this chapter is Windows Explorer – that's WINDOWS Explorer, not INTERNET Explorer. The latter is used for exploring the *Internet*. Windows Explorer is the program used for exploring the contents of your computer.

Opening Windows Explorer

There are several ways to open Windows Explorer; here are two of them.

Via the Keyboard shortcut:
Press ⊞ + E (hold down the ⊞ key and press E).
Via the All Programs Menu:
Click on **start** > **All Programs** ‣ **Accessories** ‣ **Windows Explorer**.

Windows Explorer will open in the **Folders** view, with the disk drives and folders listed in the left and right panes. The Title Bar will display the name of the item being explored – e.g. My Computer, My Documents, Local Disk (C:) or whichever folder has been selected.

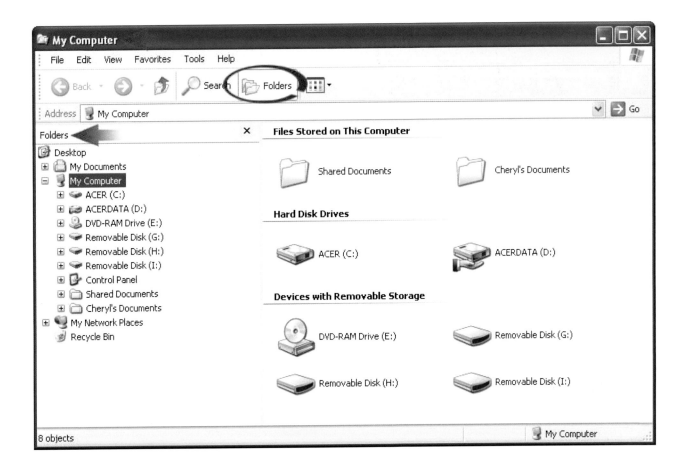

SETTING THE EXPLORER VIEW LAYOUT

Some people like to work in the **Icons** view shown above. However, to get a bird's eye view of more of the items on your computer, as well as to see other useful details about the files, we recommend you use the **Details** view.

1. On the Windows Explorer **Menu Bar**, click on **View > Details** to show a detailed list of all your drives and folders on the left. (It may already be set to this view layout.)

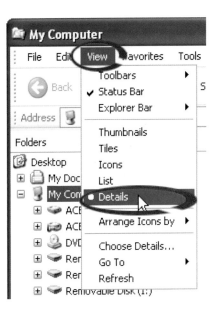

> **TIP: EXPERIMENT WITH THE OTHER VIEWS**
> Click on the other view options to see the effect, but revert to the **Details** view for the topics in this chapter. You can also click on **Arrange Icons by** ▸ to sort the icons by other criteria, and on **Choose Details...** to change the list of attributes.

2. Click on the little ⊞ **Plus** icon on the left of the **My Documents** folder (see screenshot on the right) to open the folder and display a list of any sub-folders below it. (The ⊞ **Plus** icon will change to a ⊟ **Minus** icon – see below.)

3. Click on the **My Documents** folder itself (see below), and the folders as well as any **files** stored in the My Documents folder will now be displayed in the right-hand pane.

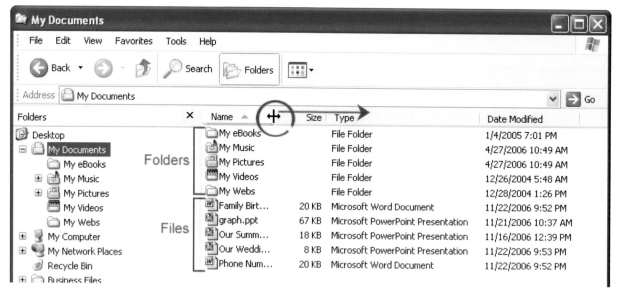

NOTE: FILE DETAILS ARE ALSO DISPLAYED IN THE RIGHT-HAND PANE

In the screenshot above, notice that when **View > Details** is selected, additional information about the files is shown in the pane on the right – size, type, date modified. If the full file name is not visible in the first column of the pane, move the pointer up to the top of that pane and onto the little grey dividing line on the right of the **Name** heading, then click and drag the divider to the right to expose more of the **Name** column.

 FILES ARE NOT DISPLAYED IN THE FOLDERS PANE
The Folders pane on the left displays only the computer drives and folders, not the files within the folders. Files are displayed in the right-hand pane and only once their folder in the left-hand pane has been clicked on to make it the active folder.

To clarify, in the screenshot below, note the following:

- The **Business Files** and the **Production** folders have had their ⊞ **Plus** icons clicked on to display their sub-folders down one level each.
- The **2006** folder's name has been clicked on to select the folder itself. Explorer therefore displays its sub-folders named **Jan to June** and **July to December** in both panes, and also displays in the right-hand pane all the **files** stored in the **2006** folder (not the files stored in the **Production** folder, because that is not the folder that has been selected).

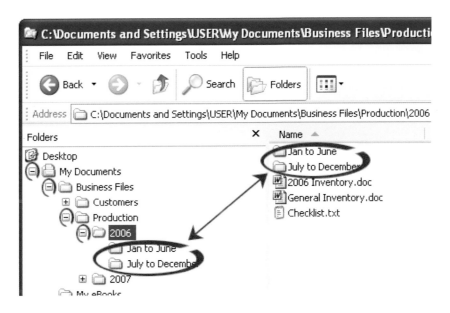

In the right-hand pane, Windows Explorer displays the sub-folders and the files stored in the folder that has been selected in the left pane, i.e. the folder named **2006.**

CREATING NEW FOLDERS

Just as a filing cabinet can have different filing drawers, each with its own filing sections in it, so too can your computer's filing system have different customized folders, each with its own sub-folders. This is a useful and logical way to manage your saved files for easy finding and opening.

Windows Explorer offers a very easy way to create a new folder, change a folder's name, and move a folder elsewhere.

1. Load **Windows Explorer** in the **Details** view.
2. In the left-hand pane click on the **My Documents** folder to select it.
3. In the Menu Bar at the top, click on **File > New ▸ Folder**.

A **New Folder** will be added in the My Documents folder and will be listed in the right-hand pane. It will be highlighted (dark) and have a border around it so that you can give it a **folder name**.

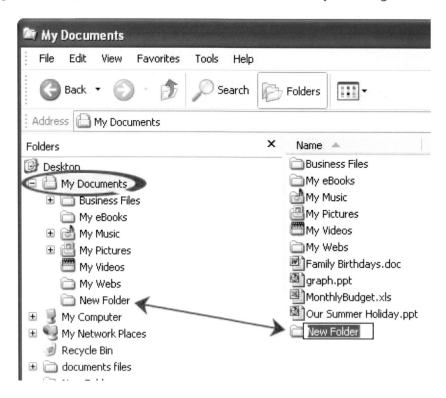

4. Type: `Computer Tutorialws` (yes, spelt that way), then press Enter , and your new folder will now bear that name.

Oops! We have a spelling mistake in that folder name. It should read Computer **Tutorials**, not **Tutorialws**. This can be fixed quite easily by renaming the folder.

RENAMING A FOLDER IN WINDOWS EXPLORER

1. Right-click on the **Computer Tutorialws** folder to open a drop-down menu.
2. Read through the menu's items to see what actions are available.
3. Click on **Rename** and note how the folder now has a border around it, as when you first created and named it. 🗀 Computer Tutorialws
4. Retype the name in the folder so that it reads **Computer Tutorials**.
5. Press Enter , or click anywhere outside the folder name and the border will disappear; the folder will now have its new, correct name.
6. On the Menu Bar at the top, click on **View > Refresh** to update the view in Windows Explorer. (You should now see the new folder listed alphabetically with the other folders under **My Documents** in both panes.)

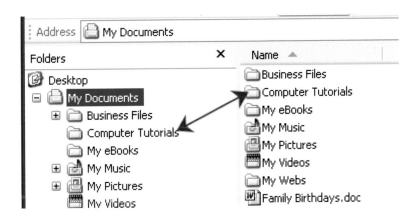

OOPS! MADE A MISTAKE?

Remember, if you 'mess up' along the way, you can press Esc to get back to where you were, and start again.

NOTE: RENAMING FILES

You can use the same procedure to rename your **files** as well.

SOME FILES MUST NOT BE RENAMED

Don't attempt to rename any program-related (application) folders or files (e.g. in program-related folders, files with .exe behind the file name) or you will create major problems for yourself because the programs won't be able to operate. You can safely change the names of document folders and document (.doc) files, as well as picture files (.jpg, .jpeg, .gif, .bmp, .tif), Excel (.xls) files, PowerPoint (.ppt or .pps) files and text (.txt) files.

CREATING FOLDERS WITHIN FOLDERS

Sometimes it's useful to create a hierarchy of folders and sub-folders in which to store related files.

TIP: ALWAYS SELECT THE MAIN FOLDER FIRST

A new folder (or 'sub-folder') will always be created within the folder that is selected and active. So, before you click on **File > New ▸ Folder**, be sure that you first click on the folder within which you want to create a new folder or sub-folder.

Here's an example of a hierarchy of folders and sub-folders:

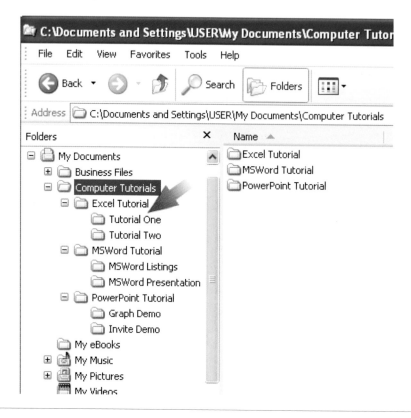

USING WINDOWS EXPLORER TO LOCATE AND OPEN FILES QUICKLY

You can open files directly from Windows Explorer without first having to load the applicable program such as Word, Excel, and so on. This is a very useful and quick method, especially if you're not sure which program was used to create the file.

1. In Windows Explorer, click on **My Documents** to display its contents in the right-hand pane – the sub-folders as well as the files – which will be listed alphabetically.

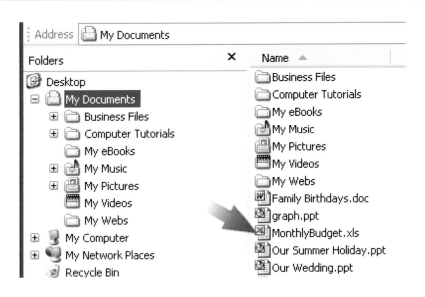

2. Double-click on the file named **MonthlyBudget** (created in Chapter 1) and Windows will automatically load **Excel** and display that workbook in the Excel window. (Windows Explorer will be sent to the background with its task icon on the Taskbar.)

NOTE: WINDOWS SELECTS THE PROGRAM NEEDED

You can open any file in this way, provided you have the applicable program installed on your computer. Windows will automatically load the appropriate program for viewing the file – for example: Word for documents, Windows Media Player for sound files, and so on. Some people open their files exclusively through Windows Explorer. It's also useful for easily seeing where you have stored your various files. Try it and see how you like using this method.

REARRANGING YOUR FOLDERS AND FILES FOR EFFICIENCY

As you add new files and folders to your system, you may want to rearrange your filing system.

Moving files

To demonstrate this, we'll move the Excel file named **MonthlyBudget** from the **My Documents** folder to the **Computer Tutorials** folder.

1. Press `Alt` + `F4` to close the Excel workbook file.
2. If Excel remains open, press `Alt` + `F4` again to close Excel too.
3. In the **left-hand pane** of the open Windows Explorer, click once on the folder named **My Documents** to select it and display its contents in the **right-hand pane**, which should include the Excel workbook file named **MonthlyBudget**.
4. In the right-hand pane click on that file named **MonthlyBudget** and hold down the mouse button while carefully moving the pointer (along with the Monthly Budget file) into the left-hand pane and onto the folder named **Computer Tutorials**, until that folder goes dark to indicate that it's been selected.
5. Now release the mouse button and the **MonthlyBudget** Excel file will be relocated from the **My Documents** folder to the **Computer Tutorials** folder.
6. If you drop it into the wrong folder, on the Menu Bar click on **Edit**, then on **Undo Move**, and try again.
7. On the Menu Bar, always click on **View > Refresh** to see the changes.

TIP: REPOSITIONING SUB-FOLDERS
You can use this same drag-and-drop method to move folders around too, as well as files. Remember, items in the left-hand pane that have a ⊞ **Plus** icon next to them contain folders and files. Folders *without* the ⊞ **Plus** icon contain files only.

NOTE: ALTERNATIVE CUT AND PASTE METHOD
An alternative method for moving folders and files is to **right**-click on the item you want to move, and in the drop-down menu that opens click on **Cut** to remove the item to the Clipboard. Then click on the destination folder you want to move it to, and press `Ctrl` + `V` to paste the item into its new location. (Alternatively, after cutting the file, **right**-click on the destination folder and in the menu that opens, click on **Paste**.)

SELECTING SEVERAL ITEMS AT ONCE

Here's a neat way to perform one action on several items at the same time. You can use it in many situations, for example:

- to select several files you wish to move or delete;
- to select and delete several e-mails from your e-mail IN folder.

There are two methods and each is applied according to the situation:

To select a range of adjacent items:

1. Hold down the Shift key and click on the first item in the list, then on the last item you want to select; all items in between will automatically be selected as well.

2. Release the Shift key and perform the action (delete, copy, drag, etc.).

To select several non-adjacent items:

1. Hold down the Ctrl key while clicking on each file you want to select.

2. Release the Ctrl key when all the required items have been selected, and perform the desired action (delete, copy, drag, etc.).

DELETING FILES OR FOLDERS IN WINDOWS EXPLORER

When you no longer need a folder or a file you can simply delete it in Windows Explorer.

1. In Windows Explorer click on the folder named **Computer Tutorials** that you created.

2. Press Del on the keyboard and, in the confirmation box that pops up, click on **OK**; the file and all its contents will be sent to the trash can (called the Recycle Bin).

3. Click on **View > Refresh** to see an updated Windows Explorer window, with the folder no longer there.

To restore the deleted folder for later use:

1. On the Menu Bar click on **Edit > Undo Delete**, and the delete action will be undone. (**Undo Delete** only works if the program hasn't been shut down and re-opened.)

2. Click on **View > Refresh** to see an updated Windows Explorer window with the folder restored to its original location.

CHECK A FOLDER'S CONTENTS BEFORE DELETING IT

When you delete a *folder*, Windows will also delete all its contents. So before deleting a folder, check what's inside it to be sure you're happy to delete all the folder's contents along with the folder itself.

THE RECYCLE BIN

The Recycle Bin – which usually has an icon on the Desktop – acts like a temporary refuse bin. When you delete a folder or file, it doesn't immediately disappear off your hard drive completely; instead it gets sent to the Recycle Bin. So the good news is that if you delete something in error you can go and retrieve it from the Recycle Bin (as long as you haven't already emptied the Recycle Bin) and restore it to where it was before you deleted it.

To keep as much free disk space as possible, it's advisable to empty the Recycle Bin periodically, which means that the deleted items will finally be removed from your computer, never to be seen again.

Restoring an item deleted in error

1. On the Desktop, **right**-click on the **Recycle Bin** icon to display a menu.
2. Click on **Open** to display the contents of the Recycle Bin.

3. Click on the items you deleted in error, to select them.
4. In the task pane on the left, click on **Restore the selected items**, and they'll all be sent back to where they were before you deleted them.

Emptying the recycle bin

1. Right-click on the Recycle Bin desktop icon, and in the menu that pops up click on **Empty Recycle Bin**.

FINDING FILES ON YOUR COMPUTER

Sometimes you may need to look for something on your computer but have no idea where it is located. You may not even remember its correct name. It may be a file, a folder, a shortcut, or even a program. To make finding things easy, Windows XP offers a Search facility that can be accessed via the Start menu or from Windows Explorer. For this procedure we'll look for the Excel file that was saved earlier. To do this we'll open the Search window from Windows Explorer.

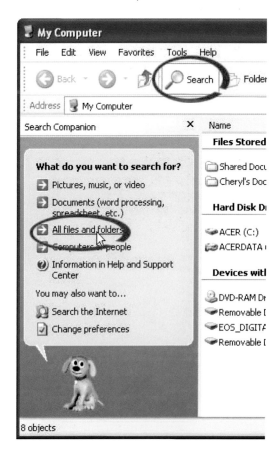

1. On the Windows Explorer Toolbar, click on the **Search** button to open the blue **Search Companion** pane on the left.
2. If you're not sure where the item is stored, click on the **All files and folders** link. (If you know for sure that it's a document or a spreadsheet, then you could narrow the search by clicking instead on the **Documents** link just above **All files and folders**.)

3. In the search criteria dialog box that opens (screenshot below), type the file name, or that part of the file name you can remember.

4. If you're not sure whether the file is stored in **My Documents**, at the **Look in:** window click on the ⌄ **down arrow** on the right.

5. In the folders list that opens, browse to **My Computer** and click on it to bring it into the **Look in:** window.

6. Click on the **Search** button to start the search.

7. When the file is found and displayed in the right-hand pane, **double**-click on it to open the file.

8. On the Taskbar, **right**-click on the **Search Results** task icon, and in the menu that opens, click on **X Close**.

TIP: CAN'T REMEMBER THE FULL FILE NAME?

When you're looking for a file but can't remember its correct name, simply type what you can remember as being the name, or just a part of the name. Windows will display all the items that contain that text in their file names.

A NOTE ABOUT 'MY COMPUTER'

Instead of using Windows Explorer, many people use My Computer to access what's available on their system, simply because it's listed on the Start menu or they have a Desktop shortcut to it. The My Computer window is a little different from the Windows Explorer window, and it has some other useful features.

1. Click on ![start], then on **My Computer** in the blue panel on the right.

The My Computer window will open with a view similar to the screenshot below. Notice the blue task panes on the left. The panes displayed will change according to what's showing in the main pane on the right. The related options for each task pane will likewise change according to which item you click on in the main pane.

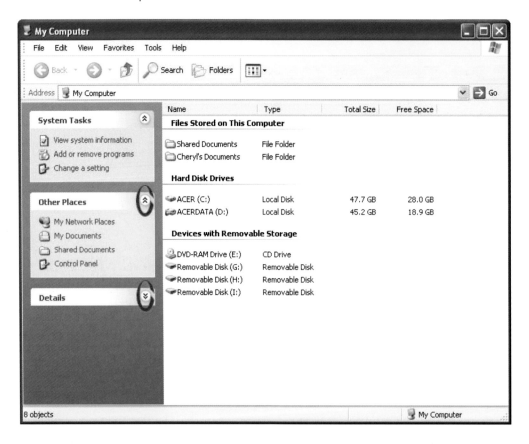

TIP: EXPANDING OR COLLAPSING A TASK PANE

Click on the ⊗ **Collapse** icon of a task pane to close the list of items in a pane – useful for revealing more task panes that may not be in view. Click on the ⊗ **Expand** icon to display the list of tasks or options in a particular pane.

CHANGING THE FOLDER DISPLAY OPTIONS

In both My Computer and Windows Explorer you can change the way folders are displayed.

1. On the Menu Bar of My Computer or Windows Explorer, click on **Tools > Folder Options...** to open the **Folder Options** dialog box.
2. Note the options available on the **General** tab.
3. Click on the **View** tab and scroll down to see what options are available there as well.

7 Keeping your system efficient

DON'T IGNORE THIS CHAPTER
As boring as this chapter's title might sound, this subject is extremely important. So do read it carefully and follow the procedures given.

GOOD HOUSEKEEPING PRACTICES

Keep the area around your computer clean and dust-free, as computers have fans that draw air inside the case to cool the internal components. If the environment where your computer is set up is dusty, vacuum the vents at the front, sides and rear of the computer on a regular basis.

Avoid eating or drinking near your computer. Spilled drinks are the number one cause of malfunctioning keyboards. If you're using a mechanical mouse with a roller ball, food crumbs may get into the mouse and cause excessive wear and tear of the rollers, necessitating cleaning or replacement of the mouse. In a nutshell, keep your workstation spotlessly clean at all times.

REGULAR SERVICING PROCEDURES

Every now and then you should clean up your hard drive by doing some minor disk maintenance. This sounds scary, but it's actually quite simple. Windows XP does it for you.

Some people say you should do a system clean weekly; others say monthly. It depends on how much you use your computer, how many files are stored on it, how much storage capacity is taken up, and so on. There are two essential procedures that should keep your computer clean and happy for a while, and improve speed:
- **Disk Cleanup:** deleting unused files and programs;
- **Disk Defragmenter:** speeding up the reading of files that have become fragmented through use, and stored in several fragments in different locations on the hard disk, making for slower access and reading by the system.

Clutter and fragmentation on the hard disk slow down a computer's performance. Using these two Windows system tools regularly will really speed up your computer.

NOTE: DIFFERENT WAYS TO ACCESS 'SYSTEM TOOLS'
There are several ways to access the various system maintenance tools, and we're showing a few of these in this section.

DISK CLEANUP: DELETING UNNEEDED FILES FROM THE HARD DISK

Disk Cleanup is for freeing up space on your hard drive. Windows stores temporary files on your system which, over time, can accumulate and take up much-needed disk space. It's a good idea to delete these frequently to free up disk space and speed up your system. Disk Cleanup also includes the option to empty the Recycle Bin.

1. Click on **start** > **All Programs** ‣ **Accessories** ‣ **System Tools** ‣ **Disk Cleanup**. If you have more than one hard drive installed, the **Select Drive** dialog box will open and ask you which drive you want to clean up.
2. If this happens, use the ⌄ **drop-down arrow** to select the drive you want to clean, (usually (**C:**) drive), then click on **OK**.

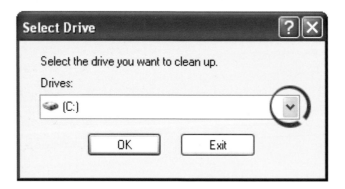

3. Wait while Disk Cleanup does some calculations before it opens the main **Disk Cleanup for (C:)** dialog box.

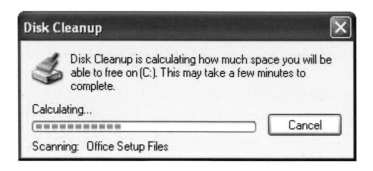

4. In the **Disk Cleanup for (C:)** dialog box that opens, tick the items to be cleaned (see suggestions in the blue TIP box).

5. Click on **OK**, and in the confirmation box that pops up, click on **Yes**.

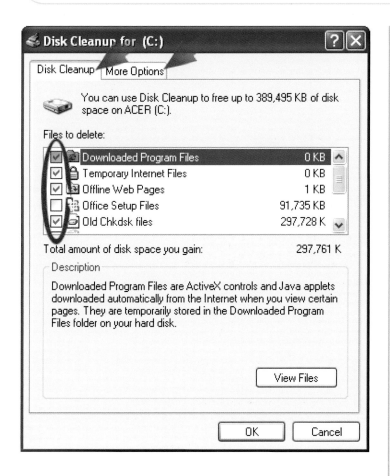

TIP: SUGGESTED FILES TO BE DELETED

Downloaded Program Files

Temporary Internet Files

Offline Web Pages

Old Chkdsk files

Microsoft Error Reporting

Temporary Files

Recycle Bin

If there are any other files that show a significant amount of disk space that would be saved, click on each one and read the description in the lower panel before deciding whether to delete them too. If you need more details, you can also click on the **View Files** button.

DISK DEFRAGMENTER: SPEEDING UP FILE ACCESS

Defragmenting is for performance improvement. With the frequent updating and deleting of files, they end up being split into separate fragments and stored bitty-bitty in different places on the hard disk. The result is that when you work with a file the system has to run around like crazy gathering up the fragments to bring the file together again so that you can work with it. Over time this can slow things down significantly.

Therefore, to keep your system running efficiently, run **Disk Defragmenter** frequently. Depending on your computer usage, this should be at least monthly.

There are a few ways in which you can access the Disk Defragmenter tool. Here are two that we suggest.

Via the All Programs menu:

Click on **start** > **All Programs** ▸ **Accessories** ▸ **System Tools**.

Via My Computer:

1. Click on **start** > **My Computer**, and **right**-click on **Local Disk (C:)**.
2. In the menu that opens, click on **Properties** to open the **Local Disk (C:) Properties** dialog box.
3. For interest, note that in the **General** tab you can see how much free disk space you have available.
4. Click on the **Tools** tab, then on the **Defragment Now...** button.

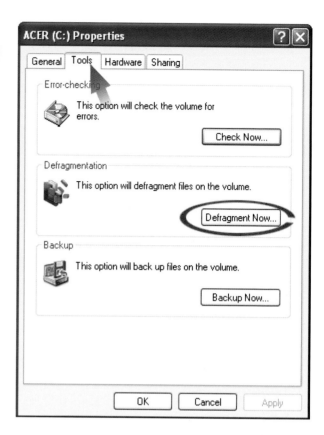

5. In the **Disk Defragmenter** window that opens next, click on the drive you wish to defragment.
6. To determine whether defragmentation is really necessary at this time, click on the **Analyze** button and follow the prompts. (If, after analysis, Windows recommends – in the little dialog box that opens – that you should defragment, then click on the **Defragment** button.)
7. To start defragmentation without analysis, click on the **Defragment** button in the main Disk Defragmenter window.

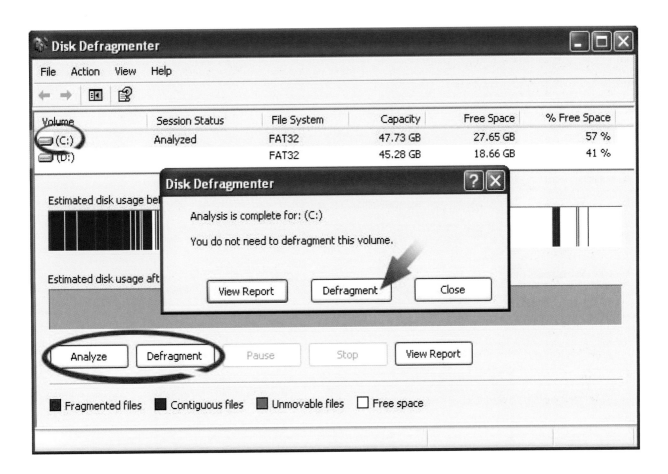

Leave the computer to do its thing until it's finished. This might take quite a while (30 to 90 minutes or even several hours, depending on how much fragmentation you have on your hard drive and on how big your hard drive is). It will tell you when it's done. Reboot (restart) your computer after defragging.

TIP: WORKING DURING DEFRAGMENTING SLOWS THINGS DOWN
Defragmenting uses resources and slows down the system. If you really need to do something urgent while defrag is in progress, it's best to click on the **Pause** button in the lower frame of the Disk Defragmenter window. When you've finished your task, click on **Continue**. A better option, however, would be to start defragmenting when you won't be needing your computer for a while.

IF YOUR COMPUTER MALFUNCTIONS

Although Windows XP is said to be more stable than earlier versions of Windows, you may nevertheless occasionally see a warning message on the screen that the program has performed an illegal operation. Or you may find that everything 'freezes' on your screen and nothing seems to be responding, sometimes not even the mouse. Don't panic. Do the following.

If the program you're using malfunctions

Sometimes a program may stop responding to keyboard or mouse commands. An error message may open too.

1. Follow any prompts in the error message that pops up.
2. Wait a while (about a minute or two), and see if things correct themselves.
3. If **Windows Task Manager** opens and states that the program is not responding, click on the **End Task** button to close the program. (You can then reload it again to continue working.)
4. If **Windows Task Manager** hasn't opened, press Ctrl + Alt + Del all at the same time, and it should open; then follow step 3 above.
5. To close Windows Task Manager, click on its ☒ **Close** button.

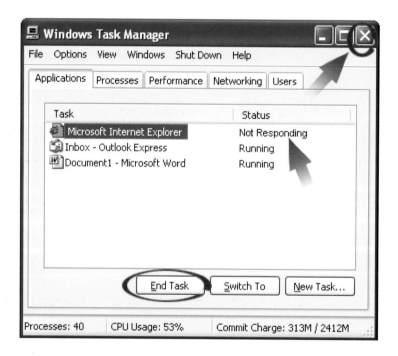

 SAVE YOUR WORK FIRST, IF POSSIBLE
If you have something very important that has not been saved, you may want to wait a while longer to see if the system eventually responds by itself. That way you won't lose any unsaved changes. If nothing happens after a while, give up and click on **End Task**.

If the program won't shut down

1. In **Windows Task Manager**, click on the **Shut Down** tab at the top, then on **Restart** and your computer should then restart (reboot); unfortunately you will lose any unsaved changes.
2. Wait while the computer restarts. (It should automatically go through the **CheckDisk** routine to fix any errors on the system.)

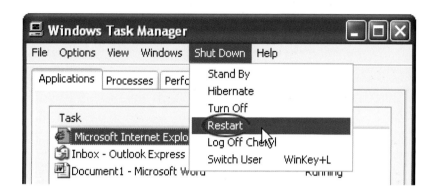

TIPS: NOTE THE OTHER MENU OPTIONS

You can also use this method to turn off the computer, log off or switch user. Note also the useful keyboard shortcut for switching user: hold down the **Windows** key and press the L key.

If everything 'freezes', and even the mouse won't respond

1. Press the **Reset** button – a small button usually located just below the Power On/Off button on the computer (underneath or in front of the machine, if it's a laptop).
2. If that won't restart the computer, then you have only one choice left: press the **Power Off** switch on your computer to turn it off.
3. Wait a minute or so to allow the hard disk to stop spinning, then press the **Power On** button to start the computer again; wait while your computer boots up and possibly performs a **CheckDisk** routine to fix any errors.

If a program starts doing strange things

1. Save your changes and exit the program, then re-open it.
2. If it still behaves strangely, or if other programs also seem to be playing up, then it's best to save your data and exit all programs; then restart the computer in the usual manner.

USING 'SYSTEM RESTORE' FOR RECENT ONGOING PROBLEMS

Sometimes the system will start playing up after there's been some change, such as installing a new program or downloading something from the Internet that is not compatible with other programs on your system. Or a virus, worm or spyware attack may have occurred and changed some of your program files or settings. Windows XP offers a function called System Restore, which allows you to restore your entire system to how it was at some earlier date, before the problems started.

1. Click on **start** > **All Programs** ▸ **Accessories** ▸ **System Tools** ▸ **System Restore**, and the System Restore dialog box will open. Read the information on the left of the box.
2. Select either **Restore my computer to an earlier time** or **Create a restore point**.
3. Click on **Next** >.
4. Click on one of the **bold** dates in the calendar to select a restore point prior to the start of the problems you've been having. (If necessary, click on the < **left arrow** next to the month to go to the previous month.)
5. Click on **Next** > to go to the confirmation box.
6. Click on **OK** to commence the restoration. (A progress bar will be displayed and then Windows will restart the computer.)
7. In the **Restoration Complete** window that should appear, click on **OK**.
8. If the System Restore did not solve your problems, repeat the process and select an even earlier **Restore Point** date.

NOTE: YOU MAY NEED TO REINSTALL SOME PROGRAMS

If you installed a program *after* the Restore Date you selected, you will need to reinstall it if you want to have access to it again. But satisfy yourself that the problems were not, in fact, as a result of that particular installation.

KEEPING YOUR WINDOWS XP SYSTEM UP TO DATE

Microsoft automatically delivers system improvements to your computer via the Internet so that you always have the latest fixes to make Windows XP work more efficiently. To check whether you have this option enabled, follow this procedure:

1. Click on **start** > **Control Panel** ▸ **System** to open the **System Properties** dialog box.
2. Click on the **Automatic Updates** tab.
3. Make sure there's a green dot in the radio button next to **Automatic (recommended)**; if not, click on it to enable it.
4. Set a time for Windows XP to download and install any updates – a time when you would normally be connected to the Internet.
5. Click on **Apply**, then on **OK**.

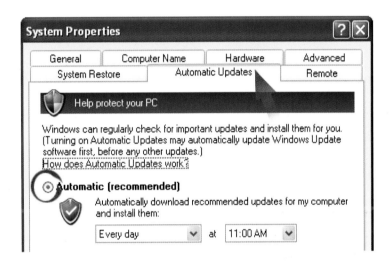

6. Click on the **Desktop** and press F1 on your keyboard to open the **Help and Support Center** window.
7. In the **Search** box type the words `automatic updates` and click on the green arrow to learn more about this topic.

Learning more

As can be seen, personal computers have a lot to offer. Our Computer Books 1 (XP) and 2 (XP) have introduced and taught many of the important aspects of using a computer as well as some of the popular programs. Yet there is still much to learn. Here are some suggestions to help you on the road ahead.

PRESSING F1 TO GET HELP

The F1 key is probably going to become your greatest friend when you need help or understanding on some aspect of using your computer or any specific application. Whatever you have up on your screen, pressing F1 will summon one or other Help window or pane.

Help with Windows XP

1. With the Desktop in view, click on the Desktop to make it active, then press F1 to call up the **Help and Support Center** (also accessible via the start menu).
2. For a guided tour of Windows XP, click on **What's new in Windows XP** and in the pane that opens click on each item in turn, starting with **Taking a tour or tutorial**; follow the prompts.
3. In the Help and Support Center window, click on the Back button to return to the previous window and select other items that interest you.

TIP: USE THE SEARCH BOX FOR SPECIFIC QUERIES

If there's something specific you want help with, type a word or phrase into the white **Search** box and click on the ➡ **Start Searching** arrow. In the next list of topics that opens, click on a link that looks as if it will take you to the information you're seeking. For additional information and notes, click on the underlined text links and shortcut icons. Note that some links will require an Internet connection because they take you to a Web site for further information.

Help with a particular program

With the program open and active on the Desktop, press F1 to open that program's **Help** window, and click on the items you need.

NOTE: HELP OPTIONS IN PROGRAMS

As with Windows XP, the Help facilities of most programs offer a **Contents window**, a **Search** box, and an **Index**, so it's pretty easy to find your way around their Help systems. Most programs have a Help button on their Toolbar as well, such as Microsoft's ⓘ **question mark**; and there is normally also a Help item in the Menu Bar. Clicking on these Toolbar or Menu Bar Help items has the same effect as pressing F1 on the keyboard.

USING THE INTERNET TO FIND ANSWERS

Another useful way of getting your questions answered is by searching for information on the Internet, and finding forums where others have similar questions that have been answered by those who've found the solutions. Some sites offer to send free hints and tips by e-mail too, often as a free service sponsored by advertisers who hope you'll click on an interesting link and order their offerings. One good search engine to use for this would be at **www.google.com**. But there are many other search engines that can be used as well.

This book's companion Web site at **www.reallyeasycomputerbooks.com** has its own forum too, where users can post their questions for others to answer. It also gives information about other books currently available in this series, such as **Really, Really, Really Easy Digital Photography for Absolute Beginners**, which not only teaches about photography itself but explains, step-by-step, all the wonderful things that can be done with the photos you tend to accumulate on your computer – processes such as editing, cropping, e-mailing, and so on. We invite you to pay a visit to our Web site.

Lastly, we do hope that you've found this book useful and enjoyable to work with. Feel free to use our Web site forum to let us have your comments.

All the best!

Index